F   Johnson, Marael.
370   Louisiana, why
.J64 a guide to Louisi
    roadside historic
    markers / Marael

WEST GEORGIA TECH LIBRARY

MW01387952

LOUISIANA
WHY STOP?

LOUISIANA
WHY STOP?

A GUIDE TO LOUISIANA'S
ROADSIDE HISTORICAL MARKERS

MARAEL JOHNSON

Gulf Publishing Company
Houston, Texas

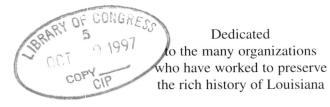

Dedicated
to the many organizations
who have worked to preserve
the rich history of Louisiana

Louisiana
Why Stop?

A Guide to Louisiana's Roadside Historical Markers

Copyright © 1996 by Gulf Publishing Company, Houston, Texas.
All rights including reproduction by photographic or electronic
process and translation into other languages are fully reserved under
the International Copyright Union, the Universal Copyright
Convention, and the Pan-American Copyright Convention.
Reproduction or use of this book in whole or in part in any manner
without written permission of the publisher is strictly prohibited.

Gulf Publishing Company
Book Division
P.O. Box 2608 □ Houston, Texas 77252-2608

10   9   8   7   6   5   4   3   2   1

Library of Congress Cataloging-in-Publication Data

Johnson, Marael.
     Louisiana, why stop? : a guide to Louisiana's roadside
historical markers / Marael Johnson.
          p.   cm.
     Includes index.
     ISBN 0-88415-924-8
     1. Historical markers—Louisiana—Guidebooks.
     2. Louisiana—Guidebooks.   3. Louisiana—History, Local.
     I. Title.   II. Title: Why stop?
     F370.J64   1996
     976.3—dc20   96-36283
                                                            CIP

Printed in the United States of America.

Contents

Acknowledgments —————————————— vi

Preface ———————————————————— vii

How to Use This Guide ——————————— ix

About Louisiana Historical Markers —————— 1

Louisiana Historical Markers
(listed alphabetically by
nearest city/town)———————————————— 2

About Louisiana African-American
  Heritage Sites ——————————————— 96

Louisiana African-American Heritage Sites
(listed alphabetically by
nearest city/town)———————————————— 97

Index ———————————————————— 150

Acknowledgments

Many thanks to Donna Fricker at the State of Louisiana Division of Historic Preservation and Troy Hayes at the State of Louisiana Division of Archives, Records Management, and History for making their files available and for their assistance and cooperation in compiling this book. Additional thanks to Jennifer Wesley for research and technical support.

Preface

Louisiana is inarguably the most exotic state in the nation. Its 48,523 square miles encompass a tasty mix of cultures from French, Spanish, and African to Native American, Caribbean, and British—not to mention a big dash of Texan over on the common border of the two states.

Louisiana's north and south sections—with Alexandria the common dividing point—are dramatically different (forget that fact and just about any local will remind you!). North Louisiana is filled with cool forests, fish-poppin' lakes, hiking trails and rolling hills, and true Southern hospitality. South Louisiana, on the other hand, is a world of its own—steamy and sultry, with cypress swamps and Cajun fiddles, jambalaya and crawfish, and the jazz and pizzazz of New Orleans (pronounce that "N'awlins").

Along the urban thoroughfares and rural roadways traversing Louisiana's cultural gumbo, and spread across 59 parishes, you will encounter most of the state's 397 official historical markers as well as 34 significant African-American heritage sites listed on the National Register of Historic Places. *Why Stop? A Guide to Louisiana's Roadside Historical Markers* allows you to keep track of what you might have missed when you just couldn't slow down (or when you never even left home!). Whether you're strapped into your car seat or just nestled in a favorite armchair, *Why Stop?* will spirit you past prehistoric digs and Indian burial grounds, gracious plantation homes and Cajun cabins, majestic cathedrals and country churches, North America's largest man-made forest and first rock salt mine, to the oldest settlement in the Louisiana Purchase and the crawfish capital of the world. Pay tribute at forts, camps, and battle sites and at theaters and dance halls. Peek into the long-ago settlements of Creoles, Acadians, Spaniards, Hungarians, and Germans. Glimpse into the lives of such diverse personalities as John James Audubon, Jim Bowie, Jean Lafitte, "Leadbelly," and Edgar Degas. See where the best seed rice and unique Perique tobacco sprouted forth. Loll along lakes, bayous, and false rivers or chug on the world's oldest continuously operated street railway. Ponder sharecropping and slave quarters as well as influential African-Americans and the rich ethnic heritage. Lose yourself in sassy New Orleans or relive Longfellow's epic poem "Evangeline" in St. Martinville.

Why Stop? can also be a helpful planning tool for your Louisiana trip, allowing you to pick and choose places of interest before leaving home. Most state and local tourist organizations can provide additional information on marker sites, and many towns and parishes publish "walking tour" maps of heritage areas.

To the best of my knowledge, the inscriptions contained herein are identical to the wording on the actual plaques. Any errors are unintentional and, upon notification, will be corrected in future editions. Additionally, markers are occasionally relocated (sometimes due to highway construction) or removed by vandals.

Enjoy *Why Stop?* on your Louisiana adventure and—as the Cajuns say—*"Laissez les bons temps rouler!"* ("Let the good times roll!").

How To Use This Guide

The marker inscriptions selected for this book have been compiled for the convenience and enjoyment of both the traveler and the history enthusiast. They occur in the order of the alphabetized cities or towns nearest them. By locating the name of the town you are approaching, you can determine the location of nearby markers by the information shown in italics. Indicated distances are measured from the nearest town within the parish in which the marker is located. The index includes 59 Louisiana parishes and lists the key persons and events responsible for the markers.

HIGHWAY AND ROAD LEGEND

US   U.S. highway
I   Interstate highway
SH   State highway

About Louisiana Historical Markers . . .

The official historic marker program, spanning the years 1951–1991, began in the Department of Commerce and Industry and was later administered by the State of Louisiana Division of Historic Preservation. The markers document the state's heritage at each location. Once approved, they were placed by the State Department of Transportation and Development and by sponsoring groups.

To qualify for an official marker, the site must meet the following criteria: It is of lasting significance to the state's history; it is of significant historical importance to the state; it is an historic trail or route; or it is a significant architectural landmark. Currently, a total of 397 markers are erected throughout the state—86 of these sponsored by private groups such as churches, civic associations, or local parishes.

Markers, made of aluminum alloy, have an arched crest in which a "pelican" symbol is superimposed on an outline of the State of Louisiana. Markers are 30 inches high by 42 inches wide, with a brown background and ivory letter faces. The name of the sponsoring group is exhibited at the bottom of the official wording. Wherever possible, private sponsors have been credited within *Why Stop?*

ABBEVILLE (Vermilion Parish)   *District 3, in town near courthouse*

Abbeville

Formerly La Chapelle. Founded in 1843 by Father Antoine Desire Megret, a native of Abbeville, France, on land purchased from Joseph LeBlanc. City incorporated by state, 1850. Became parish seat of Vermilion, 1845. Home of Louisiana Dairy Festival.

ABBEVILLE (Vermilion Parish)   *District 3, in town in front of church*

Saint Mary Magdalen Church

Four churches dedicated to Saint Mary Magdalen have stood on this site purchased from Joseph LeBlanc by Pere Megret in 1843. The present church was built in 1911 under the pastorate of Pere Laforest. [Bilingual—French on reverse.]

ABITA SPRINGS (St. Tammany Parish)   *SH 58, District 62, State Park*

Abita Springs

Old Choctaw village which derived name from nearby medicinal springs. Last Choctaw burial and execution grounds, used until about 1880, located nearby.

ALBANY (Livingston Parish)   *District 2, in front of Town Hall*

Albany, Louisiana

Town incorporated in 1953; first mayor was Grady Stewart. Railroad (B.R.H.&E.) established Albany in 1907–08. Crossed by old north-south Turnpike Road from Springfield to Natchez, MS. On portion of Spanish Headright granted to Nancy Setton in 1801.

ALEXANDRIA (Rapides Parish)   *1201 Third St.*

Alexandria Daily Town Talk

The newspaper's first edition appeared on March 17, 1883. It was the inspiration and work of two printers, Edgar Hammond McCormick and Henarie Morrison Huie. McCormick, the senior partner, was a native of St. Louis who married Huie's aunt, and they had no children.

Huie, his unmarried sister Laura, and half-brothers, Rollo C., M. Groves, and A. Hunter Jarreau, became owners of the newspaper. It was incorporated as McCormick & Co., Inc. in 1924. Descendant family members including the Dellmons, Wilsons, Smiths, O'Quins, and Hardins have been involved in the operation and management of the company.

The company, its newspaper, and an allied printing subsidiary, have been located on this and adjoining pieces of property since 1887.

News coverage focuses on Central Louisiana; carriers distribute the paper to subscribers throughout the area.

Persons employed on the newspaper's 100th Anniversary are participants in a Commemorative Trust Fund that will be shared March 17, 2033. ("Old Courthouse Square" on reverse.)

Sponsored by the Alexandria Daily Town Talk, *1991.*

ALEXANDRIA (Rapides Parish)   *Downtown, in front of library*
Alexandria Library

This site, located in the town's center square, was set aside for public use on the original town plat commissioned by Alexander Fulton in 1805. The building was constructed solely for advancement of culture and learning in 1907 by Caldwell Brothers, Contractors, and Crosby & Henkel of New Orleans, Architects. It replaced an earlier library burned by Gen. Nathaniel Banks' federal troops May 13, 1864. Area businessman S.S. Bryan matched a $10,000.00 grant from Pittsburgh philanthropist Andrew Carnegie. The funds were given for a free public library with the stipulation that the City provide a "site and maintenance forever." An accepting ordinance was adopted by Alexandria's Board of Aldermen May 7, 1907. The Alexandria City Council in 1971 adopted a resolution designating the building as the Alexandria Historical and Genealogical Library and Museum. It was restored as a Bicentennial project. Through the date of the placing of this marker, 1990, the building remains in public ownership as the City's only public building over 75 years old used for its original purpose. It was placed on the National Register of Historic Places January 19, 1989.

Sponsored by the City of Alexandria.

ALEXANDRIA (Rapides Parish) *In Pineville, at cemetery*

Alexandria National Cemetery

The Alexandria National Cemetery, Pineville, was authorized by an Act of Congress on February 22, 1867, and the United States, through the Secretary of War, took possession April, 1871, of this property from the Succession of Francois Poussan. The parcel containing 8.24 acres was valued by United States District Judge W.B. Woods in the amount of $1,200.00, pursuant to an order of the United States District Court signed May 21, 1875.

The cemetery was originally enclosed with a picket fence, later replaced with a brick wall in 1870. Lodge built in 1879, rebuilt in 1931. Sun porch added in 1938 by W.P.A. labor. Flag mound and flagstaff replaced in November 1950.

Initially, there were 1,378 interments, 837 unknown, 507 known. Later, the following transfers were made to three common graves. 1,514 unknown soldiers originally interred in Fort Brownsville, Texas, as casualties of the Civil War were interred in one grave.

In a second grave, 25 unknown soldiers were transferred from post and private cemeteries near old Fort Jesup, Louisiana.

A third grave bears the remains of 16 unknown soldiers originally interred at Fort Ringo, Texas. During World War II, five German prisoners of war were given interment.

In 1973, the responsibility for operation of the cemetery was transferred to the Veterans Administration Hospital.

ALEXANDRIA (Rapides Parish) *In front of Bolton House*

The James Wade Bolton House

When Alexandria was first surveyed as a town in 1805, this site was one-half block south of the public square. In 1899, James Wade Bolton, of the prominent Alexandria banking family, acquired this property. The house is exemplary of Queen Anne Revival architecture in Louisiana. Showing traditional regional influences, such as long-leaf yellow pine framing and a raised on-pier foundation, it features twice the number of principal rooms usually found in such fine residences. Additional features include fifteen-foot ceilings, oak paneling, an extravagant use of windows, and an expansive curving front veranda supported by Ionic columns. Directly across St. James Street was the house of his father, George Washington Bolton, a pioneer financier and patriarch of the Bolton family in Central Louisiana. In 1979, the Bolton house was donated to the city of Alexandria by the Bolton family as a center for regional arts and crafts. At that time, it was renamed "River Oaks Square."

Sponsored by Central Cities Development Corporation.

ALEXANDRIA (Rapides Parish)   *In town*

City of Alexandria

Unnamed during the colonial period, Alexandria's beginnings as the major city in Central Louisiana are traced to c. 1797, when the "seat of justice" for Rapides Post was transferred from the north to the south bank of Red River. By 1799, the greater percentage of the population was located here. Growth was rapid, spurred by the introduction of the cotton gin in 1800 by Alexander Fulton. Within two years, Fulton had begun clearing land, opening roads, and in 1805, Frederick Walther, Fulton's surveyor, laid out the "Town of Alexandria." The plat contained eighty square blocks between present-day Jackson Street, Tenth Street, Overton Street, and the river, surrounding a public square. Tradition holds that the town's name honored a young Fulton daughter. Following the Louisiana Purchase of 1803, Alexandria became the seat of justice when an act creating Rapides County became law on April 10, 1805. Trade, business, and agriculture gained greatly with the advent of steamboat service. In late December 1814, the first steamboat, *Enterprise,* captained by Henry Miller Shreve, docked at Alexandria.

In 1818, the State Legislature granted Alexandria a charter. Because of the rapids immediately to the north, the town was the head of navigation for Red River from July to January. This created growth as a shipping point, with such institutions as newspapers (1810), semi-public schools (1818), banks (1823), and libraries (1824) being founded.

During the decades preceding the Civil War, Alexandria became the most important trade and social center for the plantation system in Central Louisiana. As a result of agricultural activity, the first railroad west of the Mississippi was constructed in 1837 by Ralph Smith-Smith, with the depot located at Courthouse Square.

Alexandria was the focus of military activity in Louisiana during the last two years of the Civil War. The town was designated Headquarters for the Confederate Trans-Mississippi Department by order of Lieutenant General E. Kirby Smith on March 7, 1863. Two months later, Alexandria was briefly occupied by a raiding Union force under the command of General Nathaniel P. Banks supported by naval forces under Admiral David D. Porter.

A second invasion of the Red River valley in April 1864 by the Union under the same officers was repelled by Confederate forces under the command of General Richard Taylor. In their retreat, Union troops burned Alexandria, destroying all courthouse and municipal records; the date was Friday, May 13, 1864.

Sponsored by the City of Alexandria.

ALEXANDRIA (Rapides Parish)   *3601 Bayou Rapides Rd.*
Kent Plantation House

Kent House, the oldest known standing structure in central Louisiana, was built by Pierre Baillio, completed in 1800. Baillio constructed the house on land received through a Spanish land grant circa 1794.

ALEXANDRIA (Rapides Parish)   *On DeSoto St., next to Hotel Bentley*
Louisiana Maneuvers

In 1940, Lt. Gen. Stanley D. Embrick of the U.S. Army Fourth Corps Area, Atlanta, Ga., selected central Louisiana as site of training maneuvers to prepare American forces for possible involvement in war in Europe. Louisiana's 1941 maneuvers were the Army's largest peacetime training exercise. Approximately 400,000 troops were divided into armies of two imaginary countries: "Kotmk" (Kansas, Oklahoma, Texas, Missouri, and Kentucky) and "Almat" (Arkansas, Louisiana, Mississippi, Alabama, and Tennessee), supposedly at war over Mississippi River navigation rights. These maneuvers allowed Army strategists to test conventional defenses attacked by armored vehicles. Maj. Gen. George Patton's tanks pushed back conventionally-armed defenders but failed to achieve a spectacular victory. Army commanders also encountered reconnaissance and troop supply problems expected in battlefield conditions and thus had several months to formulate solutions before the U.S. entered World War II. The Army conducted smaller-scale maneuvers in 1942 and 1943 in the same area, but canceled 1944 exercises to allow troops to participate in the D-Day invasion of Europe. In addition to Patton, military leaders who visited central Louisiana during the maneuvers included Joseph Stilwell, Dwight Eisenhower, Omar Bradley, Mark Clark, and J. Lawton Collins. Many of these headquartered at the Hotel Bentley.

Sponsored by Johnson Brown Post 1736—V.F.W.

ALEXANDRIA (Rapides Parish)   *In the downtown minipark*
Thomas Courtland Manning
1825–1887

On this site in 1906, the City Library known as the Manning Memorial Library was opened, named in honor of a 19th-century resident who served his State and his Nation. Hundreds of his personal volumes were donated to this library, which ceased operation a year or so later.

Born in Edenton, North Carolina, he became an attorney by "reading-for-the-law," *Albamarie Sentinel* editor, educator at Edenton Academy, and Master of the Equity Court, Chowas County.

In 1855, he moved his family to Alexandria. Their residence was eight blocks west, bounded by Second, Third, Madison, and St. Anne streets, and faced Red River.

His major accomplishments in life were: Member of first Board of Supervisors for La. Seminary (LSU); Adjutant General of La.—C.S.A—1863–1864; Assoc. Justice of La. Supreme Court—C.S.A—1864–1865; Chief Justice of the La. Supreme Court—1877–1880; Assoc. Justice of La. Supreme Court—1882–1886; U.S. Minister Plenipotentiary to Mexico 1886–1887.

ALEXANDRIA (Rapides Parish)   *1201 Third St.*
Old Courthouse Square

Rapides was one of the twelve original counties created when the Territory of Orleans was divided in 1805. Records are not available about early courthouses on this square, which was reserved for public use by the town's founder in a plat of February 1, 1805.

A new courthouse built in 1859 was destroyed by fire on May 13, 1864, by Federal troops evacuating Alexandria in retreat down the Red River. Legal records and much of the town were burned. Hard times delayed the replacement courthouse until 1873. A parish jail was built on the Lee Street corner in 1899.

The last courthouse on this site, costing $75,000, was occupied in 1904. In 1940, a new, still existing courthouse was built on Murray Street. The jail was soon demolished; the old deteriorating courthouse was razed in 1957. The square was later acquired by McCormick & Co. for use by the *Town Talk*. (*Alexandria Daily Town Talk* on reverse.)

Sponsored by the Alexandria Daily Town Talk.

ALEXANDRIA (Rapides Parish) *Next to approach ramp to Pineville Bridge, between Main St. and Red River levee*

Old Rapides Bank Building

This structure was built on property that once belonged to Alexander Fulton. He had acquired it at the end of the 18th century from Marguerite Cecile Christophe Varrangue. Various persons occupied this site until it was acquired by Rapides Bank in two purchases dated February 26, 1897, and February 5, 1898. The Bank moved to this new location when it was ten years old, in September 1898, under the leadership of its first president, Col. George Washington Bolton. The original building featured Renaissance Revival detailing, but in 1914, it was remodeled in the neoclassical style by the noted New Orleans architectural firm of Favrot & Livaudais. The impressive three-bay limestone facade is articulated with engaged colossal Tuscan columns, arched windows, and a balustraded entablature. Following the remodeling, a series of flood control set-back levees enveloped all of adjacent First (Front) Street and one-half of each block between First and Second (Main) streets. Rapides Bank occupied this site until 1954, when it moved two blocks south. This structure was donated in 1982 by the Bank to the Alexandria Museum.

Sponsored by Central Cities Development Corporation.

ALEXANDRIA (Rapides Parish) *Corner of Main and Murray sts.*

Rapides Parish Governors

Four 19th-century Rapides Parish residents served Louisiana as governor.

Joseph Marshall Walker (1784–1856), a Bayou Rapides cotton planter, was governor 1850–1853—the first to be installed in the newly-designated Baton Rouge capital. During his administration, improvements were made in water and railway transportation, telegraph lines built, levees and drainage improved, and a state banking system established.

Thomas Overton Moore (1804–1877), a Bayou Robert planter, was governor 1860–1864, including the two-month period of independence when Louisiana had seceded from the Union but had not joined the Confederacy. During his term, the capital was twice moved to escape the Federal troops' invasion.

James Madison Wells (1808–1899), a Bayou Boeuf plantation owner, was elected lieutenant governor of federally-occupied Louisiana in 1864 and served as governor from 1865 to 1867. He sought reconciliation between Unionists and Secessionists.

Newton Crain Blanchard (1849–1922), born and reared on Bayou Jean de Jean, was governor 1904–1908. His administration was known for progressive reform.

Sponsored by the City of Alexandria.

ALEXANDRIA (Rapides Parish)   *SH 18, District 2, in town*

State Seminary of Learning and Military Academy

Provided for by Constitution of 1845 with funds from fed. land grants. Opened, 1860; closed during Civil War; reopened, 1865. Burned, 1869; moved to Institute for Deaf, Dumb, Blind, Baton Rouge. Became Louisiana State University, 1870.

ALEXANDRIA (Rapides Parish)   *In town*

St. Francis Xavier Cathedral Complex

When Poste du Rapides was established in Pineville, the Catholic mission of St. Louis des Apalachees was founded. Mass was said in private homes in the new town of Alexandria. A chapel built in 1817 was the first church of any denomination in this city. St. Francis Xavier Church was built in 1834 on Front Street. Rev. Leonard Menard envisioned a larger place of worship. The cornerstone of the present edifice was laid on the Feast of St. Francis Xavier, December 3, 1895. A few weeks later the original church burned. The first Mass was celebrated in this Gothic Revival structure November 27, 1899. Sand for mortar was dug from the Red River bed and floors of native pine were laid. In 1907 the belfry was added; the clock installed the following year. The Rectory, first built in 1896, was extensively renovated in 1930. St. Francis Xavier Academy, erected in 1897, was remodeled and enlarged in 1907. Bishop Cornelius Van de Ven petitioned Rome to transfer the See city from Natchitoches to centrally located Alexandria. Thus, on August 6, 1910, St. Francis Xavier Church became the Cathedral. These 3 buildings are now listed on the National Register of Historic Places as the Cathedral Complex.

Sponsored by Central Cities Development Corporation.

ALEXANDRIA (Rapides Parish) *US 71/167, District 8, near town*
Thos. Overton Moore

Leader in the secession movement and Confederate Governor of Louisiana 1860–1864. This is site of Mooreland, his plantation home, burned by Banks' retreating Union Army in Spring, 1864.

ALGIERS (Orleans Parish) *District 2, in Aurora Gardens*
Battle of New Orleans
West Side

Here on Jourdan Plantation, American forces under General D. B. Morgan defended west side of river against British forces on January 8, 1815. Original earthwork still in Aurora on campus of Junior University of New Orleans in Algiers.

AMITE (Tangipahoa Parish) *District 62, in town*
The Church of the Incarnation—Protestant Episcopal

The Church, incorporated in 1871, was admitted into Union. Heirs of John M. Bach donated the present site. In 1872 the Rev. Herman Cope Duncan, missionary to this area, became the first rector.

ARABI (St. Bernard Parish) *In town*
First Ward Justice Courthouse and Jail

Designed by Henry Daboval and built by J. C. Bourg in 1911. Court was held here until 1923 by Justices of the Peace. Three small jail cells remained occupied through 1939. The jail was restored in 1985.

Sponsored by St. Bernard Historical Society and St. Bernard Parish Police Jury.

ATHENS (Claiborne Parish) *District 4, near town*
Russellville

350 yards east. Site of parish seat of Claiborne Parish from soon after the parish's creation in 1828 until 1836. Named for Samuel Russell, who donated the land. First parish courthouse and jail constructed here.

AUDUBON PARK (Orleans Parish)   *District 2, in town*
Bore Plantation

This site 1781–1820 Plantation of Jean Etienne Bore (1741–1820) First Mayor of N. O. 1803–1804. Here Bore first granulated sugar in 1795. Purchased for park in 1871. Site of world's Industrial and Cotton Centennial Exposition 1884–1885.

AVERY ISLAND (Iberia Parish)   *District 3, in town*
First Rock Salt Mine

Salt evaporated from brine springs on Avery Island since 1791. On May 4, 1862, workmen enlarging these springs to produce more salt for the Confederacy hit solid salt at a depth of 16 feet. Mining operations, the first of this type in North America, were begun and continued until destruction of the salt works on April 17, 1863, by Union forces.

BAINS (West Feliciana Parish)   *US 61, District 61, near town*
Afton Villa

19th Century Gardens, site of famed antebellum mansion built in 1849 by David Barrow, once wealthiest planter in W. Feliciana; destroyed by fire in 1963. Tomb of Alexander Barrow, U.S. Senator from La. in 1840s, in family cemetery.

BALDWIN (St. Mary Parish)   *US 90, District 3, in town*
Chitimacha Indians

Four miles north are the remnants of once forceful Indian tribe. Decimated by War with French, 1706–18, many became slaves to colonists. The Chitimacha were finest basket weavers of time.

BARATARIA (Jefferson Parish)   *In town*
Poblacion de Barataria
(Barataria Settlement)

To guard New Orleans, Spain in 1779 settled 56 families from the Canary Islands on lands starting at Crown Point. Flooding by the Mississippi River forced most of the settlers to relocate in 1782. Efforts to resettle failed and finally ceased in 1802, but scattered descendants have preserved the "Isleno" culture to the present day in nearby areas.

Sponsored by Jefferson Historical Society of Louisiana.

BASTROP (Morehouse Parish)   *US 165, District 5, in front of Snyder Museum*

Luther E. Hall

Born 1869 near Bastrop. State Senator, 1898–1900; State District Judge, 1900–1906; State Appellate Judge, 1906–1911; Louisiana Governor, 1912–1916; Assistant Attorney General, 1918–1921. Died 1921 and buried in Bastrop cemetery.

BASTROP (Morehouse Parish)   *District 5, on grounds of Bastrop Jr. High West*

Morehouse Parish Training School

Site of first school built for Morehouse Parish blacks. Built 1916 through efforts of parish school board and several Bastrop blacks. Subsequent buildings housed Morehouse High School until 1969.

Sponsored by Alumni, Faculty, Students, and Friends.

BASTROP (Morehouse Parish)   *US 165, District 5, in town*

Point Pleasant

Here in 1775, Francois Bonaventure, French Indian trader, built a house on 2,000-acre tract and named the plantation "Old Cabbins." He was well established when Don Juan Filhoil came into this region.

BATON ROUGE (East Baton Rouge Parish) *District 61, corner of State Capitol Dr. and N. Fifth St.*

Arsenal Museum

This building, erected c. 1835 as a powder magazine for a U.S. Army Post and Arsenal which used this area from 1810–1885, except in 1861–1862 when held by the Confederacy. In 1962 this building was restored and the museum established.

BATON ROUGE (East Baton Rouge Parish)   *District 61, on Front Street*
Baton Rouge
State Capital named by Iberville 1699 from Indian name *Iti Humma,* Red Pole. Village settled 1721. British, 1763–1779; Spanish 1779–1810. Republic of West Florida, 1810. Home of Louisiana State University.

BATON ROUGE (East Baton Rouge Parish)   *US 61, District 61, near town*
Bayou Manchac (Iberville River)
It marked the boundary between areas possessed by Great Britain and Spain 1763–1779, and Spain and the United States 1803–1810.

BATON ROUGE (East Baton Rouge Parish)   *Intersection of Highland Rd. and South Blvd.*
Highland Road
Once called High Lands Road, this dirt roadway, cleared under Spanish rule, was lined by 1858 with sugar and cotton plantations. Beginning at South Boulevard, it extended southeastwardly approx. nine miles along Bayou Fountaine.
Sponsored by the City of Baton Rouge—Parish of East Baton Rouge.

BATON ROUGE (East Baton Rouge Parish)   *District 61, on Front Street*
Pentagon Buildings
Constructed 1819–1822 to house U.S. troops. Used as a garrison from 1822–1977 except from 1861–62 when held by Confederates. From 1886–1925 these buildings and grounds were the site of Louisiana State University.

BATON ROUGE (East Baton Rouge Parish)   *District 61, South Stadium Rd., LSU Campus*
Sugar Kettle
Used by Jean Etienne de Bore in 1795 to granulate sugar from Louisiana cane for the first time, thus revolutionizing Louisiana's economy. The kettle was later bought by planter John Hill and given to Louisiana State University.

BAYOU GOULA (Iberville Parish) *SH 1, District 61, in town*
Bayou Goula

Mugulasha Indian village captured by Bayougoulas. In 1699 Bienville here found de Tonti's letter of 1686 to LaSalle. Father Paul Du Ru built first chapel in Louisiana near village in 1700.

BAYOU LAFOURCHE (Assumption Parish) *District 61, near Napoleonville*
Valenzuela Dans La Fourche

Founded under Spanish rule c. 1778 by Canary Islanders, later joined by Acadians and others. Post believed to have been on site of "Belle Alliance Plantation," 841-acre grant to don Juan Vives, early Spanish physician, officer in the Galvez Expedition.

BELLE CHASSE (Plaquemines Parish) *River Road, District 2*
Fort St. Leon

Designed by De Verges and garrisoned in 1754, but abandoned in 1792. Because of strategic value it was rebuilt by Latour in 1808 and garrisoned to defend New Orleans. Destroyed by Adm. Farragut during Civil War in advance up the river.

BELLEVUE (Bossier Parish) *SH 157, District 4, in town*
Bossier Parish Court—Police Jury

Historic site of Freedonia, where first session of Bossier Parish court was held September 25, 1843; presiding was Judge W. K. Beck. Site later named Society Hill, then Bellevue. First Police Jury meeting was held about two miles northeast on site of Bodcau Bayou Dam.

BERNICE (Union Parish) *District 5, near town*
Old Shiloh Community

Two Louisiana governors were born nearby—William W. Heard (1900–1904) and Ruffin G. Pleasant (1916–1920). Post office established 1851 and discontinued 1906. Site of Concord Institute, a Baptist college, c. 1877–1884.

BERWICK (St. Mary Parish)   *In town*
Twin City Gospel Temple

Originally the Methodist Episcopal Church. Built in 1886 by sugar cane plantation owner Capt. John N. Pharr and wife Henrietta. They donated the church building and land to the Methodists in 1899.
Sponsored by Twin City Gospel Temple.

BIG BEND (Avoyelles Parish)   *SH 451, at bridge*
Sarto Old Iron Bridge

Prior to 1913, floodwaters from the nearby Mississippi, Atchafalaya, and Red rivers frequently forced the evacuation of people, livestock, and property in the Big Bend area. The Avoyelles Parish Police Jury in 1915 authorized the construction of an elevated permanent bridge over Bayou des Glaises at Sarto Lane. The steel truss swing bridge was completed in 1916 for vehicular and boat traffic. This parish landmark is a rare surviving example of its type and is honored by being the first bridge in Louisiana listed on the National Register of Historic Places.

Sarto Old Iron Bridge

Jusqu'en 1913, les crues du Mississippi, tout proche, et des rivieres Red (Rouge) et Atchafalaya obligeaient frequemment hommes et betail a fuir la zone dite du "Big Bend." En 1915, le Conseil de la Paroisse des Avoyelles autorisa la construction d'un pont, enjambant le Bayou des Glaises au lieu dit "Sarto Lane." Sa construction fut achevee en 1916, et le pont servait a la fois pour le passage des vehicules et des bateaux. Cet ouvrage historique est l'un des derniers exemples de ce type de construction, et fut le premier pont de l'Etat de Louisiane a figurer sur le Registre des Monuments Nationaux.

BISLAND (St. Mary Parish)   *District 3, near Calumet Bridge*
Battle of Bisland
April 12–13, 1863

Gen. Nathaniel P. Banks' Union army attacked Gen. Dick Taylor's Confederate forces entrenched at Fort Bisland. Confederates repulsed each attack, but post evacuated when Union flanking force landed at Irish Bend.

BOGALUSA (Washington Parish)   *District 62, in town*
Bogalusa's Birthplace

City was born in 1906 just west of here on Bogue Lusa Creek bank when tents were set for 1st campsite of Great Southern Lumber Co. Portable sawmill was erected to cut lumber to build town and what became world's largest sawmill.

BOGALUSA (Washington Parish)   *District 62, in town*
Hand-planted Forest

Among earliest reforestation efforts in U.S. occurred here in 1920. Since then, Crown Zellerback Corp. and its predecessors have planted 161,731 acres in creating largest man-made forest on North American continent.

BOGALUSA (Washington Parish)   *District 62, in town*
Largest Sawmill Site

Just east of here stood Great Southern Lumber Co. (1908–38). Founders F. H. and C.W. Goodyear chose city and mill sites May 15, 1906. Sawmill began operations Sept. 1, 1908, with million board test daily capacity, making it world's largest.

BOGALUSA (Washington Parish)   *District 62, in town*
Union Avenue Baptist Church

Organized by 11 charter members in a log cabin at Pool's Bluff in 1855. Was first organized church, and its building housed first school in Bogalusa. Several log buildings also used as schools were occupied until 1874, when first lumber church was built. Moved to present location in 1913.

BOSSIER CITY (Bossier Parish)   *SH 3, District 4, in town*
Bossier Shed Road

The Shed Road, completed in 1880 by Judge John Watkins of Minden, LA., was old Louisiana's most unique road. The shed covering the road was continuous for nine miles from Red River in Bossier Parish to Red Chute. It was abandoned after the coming of the first railroad some fifteen years later.

BOUTTE (St. Charles Parish) *District 2, in town*
Skirmish of Boutte Station

Union train with sixty men ambushed by Confederate force of Louisiana militia and volunteers on September 4, 1862. Train escaped to New Orleans. Fourteen Union soldiers killed and twenty-two wounded in the skirmish.

BRAITHWAITE (Plaquemines Parish) *SH 39, District 2, in town*
English Turn

So named because in this bend, Sept. 1699, Bienville, coming downstream, met the British who had come up river to choose site for a settlement. Bienville convinced Captain Lewis Banks that the territory was in possession of the French. Early concessions were established in the vicinity.

BREAUX BRIDGE (St. Martin Parish) *SH 31, District 3, in town*
Breaux Bridge

Founded 1859. Long recognized for its culinary artistry in the preparation of crawfish. The 1958 Louisiana Legislature officially designated Breaux Bridge "La Capitale Mondiale De L'Ecrevisse" in honor of its centennial year.

BRIDGE CITY (Jefferson Parish) *District 2, in town, River Front near Westwego*
Magnolia Lane

Area known as Nine Mile Point; site of Fortier Plantation and one of area's first schools, churches, and later site of WWI commissary. Once the home of Francois Quinet, Sr., statesman and developer of early New Orleans; nearby was site of Fort Banks which blockaded River during Civil War.

BROUSSARD (Lafayette Parish) *302 W. Main St.*
St. Cecilia School

Dedicated August 25, 1909, by Fr. Arthur Drossaerts, Pastor of Sacred Heart Church in Broussard, and opened on September 15, 1909, with an enrollment of seventy students. Accredited as an elementary and secondary school by the State Department of Education in 1922. The High School

Department closed in 1964 by order of the Bishop of Lafayette in a movement to consolidate Catholic high schools in Lafayette Parish. The Sisters of Divine Providence administered the school until 1974. The main building was listed on the National Register of Historic Places, March 14, 1983.

BRUSLY (West Baton Rouge Parish) *Off SH 1, District 61, between Port Allen and Plaquemine*

The Back Brusly Oak

Member Louisiana Live Oak Society. Estimated to be over 330 years old in the Bicentennial Year of 1976. Community gathering place for many years.

BUNKIE (Avoyelles Parish) *US 71, District 8, in town*

Epps House

Built in 1852 by Edwin Epps. Originally located near Holmesville on Bayou Boeuf about three miles away. From 1843 to 1853, Epps, a small planter, owned Solomon Northup, author of famous slave narrative *Twelve Years A Slave.*

BURNSIDE (Ascension Parish) *River Road, District 61*

Bocage Plantation

Built in 1801 by Marius Pons Bringier as wedding gift for daughter Fanny, who married Christophe Colomb, a French refugee. Remodeled by Architect James Dakin in 1837. Restored by Dr. and Mrs. E. G. Kohlsdorf 1941.

BURNSIDE (Ascension Parish) *River Road, District 61*

Houmas House

Houmas Indian land grant sold to Conway and Latil in 1774. Sold to Revolutionary War hero Wade Hampton 1811. Greek Revival mansion built by John Smith Preston in 1840. Restored by Dr. George Crozat in 1940.

BURNSIDE (Ascension Parish) *River Road, District 61*
L'Hermitage

Greek Revival mansion built by Marius Pons Bringier as wedding gift for his son Michel Douradou, who named the house for General Andrew Jackson's home in Tennessee. The Jacksons visited here in the 1820s.

BURTVILLE (East Baton Rouge Parish) *SH 30, District 61, in town*
English Manchac

Part of West Florida. Now in East Baton Rouge Parish. Bayou Manchae starting at the Mississippi River through the lakes was main travel route to Gulf of Mexico, 1699–1799. Site of Fort Bute captured by Spanish Governor Bernardo De Galvez, 1779.

BURTVILLE (East Baton Rouge Parish) *SH 30, District 61, in town*
Spanish Manchac

Part of Isle of Orleans—now in Iberville Parish. Bayou Manchac boundary line, 1763–79, between British West Florida and Spanish Louisiana. Flag raised by Governor de Ulloa. Site of Spanish fort built at the urge of Don Francisco Bouligny.

CADDO LAKE (Caddo Parish) *District 4, on lake shore*
First Over-Water Oil Well

The world's first over-water oil well was completed in Caddo Lake in 1911. The Ferry Lake No. 1 was erected by Gulf Refining Co. The well bottomed at 2,185 feet and produced 450 barrels per day.
Sponsored by Gulf Oil Corporation and Caddo-Pine Island Oil and Historical Society.

CADDO-PINE ISLAND FIELD (Caddo Parish) *District 4, at well site*
First Oil Well in Caddo-Pine Island Field

The first oil well in Caddo-Pine Island Field completed 1905 by Savage Brothers and Morrical. It was the first in North Louisiana and opened up the field for the Great Caddo-Pine Island Oil Boom.
Sponsored by Caddo-Pine Island Oil and Historical Society.

CAMP BEAUREGARD (Rapides Parish)

At the camp

Camp Beauregard

WORLD WAR I

Camp Beauregard, activated in July 1917 and named for General Pierre Gustave Toutant Beauregard, was the home of the 39th Infantry Division of Arkansas, Mississippi, and Louisiana.

WORLD WAR II

Reactivated as a federal facility in September 1940, the post served as the focal point for the army maneuvers of 1940–1942. On 20 October 1940, the U.S. Army V Corps was activated here. By June 1941, Camp Beauregard was the hub of a military complex that included Camps Claiborne, Livingston, and Polk. Units activated or inducted into federal service at these posts during the period 1940–1942 included the following:

Camp Beauregard

107th Air Corps Observation Squadron	Michigan NG	15 Oct 1940
V Corps		20 Oct 1940
106th Cavalry (H-Mech)	Illinois NG	25 Nov 1940
109th Air Corps Observation Squadron	Minnesota NG	10 Feb 1941
3d Armored Division		15 Apr 1941
122nd Air Corps Observation Squadron	Louisiana NG	01 Oct 1941

Camp Claiborne

151st Engineer Regiment (C)	Alabama NG	27 Jan 1941
34th Infantry Division	Iowa NG	10 Feb 1941
	Minnesota NG	
	North Dakota NG	
	South Dakota NG	
82d Airborne Division	(Redesignated)	15 Aug 1941
101st Airborne Division	(Redesignated)	15 Aug 1941

Camp Livingston

32d Infantry Division	Wisconsin NG	15 Oct 1940
	Michigan NG	

Dedicated to the men and women of the Armed Services that served at these installations and to the people of Central Louisiana for their support.

The Louisiana National Guard

CAMP CLAIBORNE (Rapides Parish)

At site in Kisatchie National Forest

Camp Claiborne

(Activated Oct. 1940—Deactivated Dec. 1945)

Camp Claiborne was named for William C. C. Claiborne, first governor of the State of Louisiana. The Camp was part of the 8th Service Command. It was also home for the U.S. Army's 34th Infantry Division, the first American force sent to the European theater. The Camp's 23,000 acres were also the center of the famous "Louisiana Maneuvers," which were the largest peacetime war games ever conducted. Almost 500,000 American troops trained here between 1940–1945. When Congress deactivated the Camp, use of the land was returned to the U.S. Forest Service.
Sponsored by Kisatchie National Forest.

CAMP LIVINGSTON (Rapides Parish)

At site in Kisatchie National Forest

Camp Livingston

(Activated Oct. 1940—Deactivated Nov. 1945)

Camp Livingston was named for Louisiana statesman Robert R. Livingston. The Camp was part of the 8th Service Command and was home for the U.S. Army's 32nd Infantry Division. Camp Livingston's 47,000 acres were part of the famous "Louisiana Maneuvers," which were the largest peacetime war games ever held. The 44,000 men stationed here during WWII fought in both the European and Pacific theaters. When the Camp was deactivated in 1945, use of the land was returned to the U.S. Forest Service.
Sponsored by Kisatchie National Forest.

CARENCRO (Lafayette Parish)

2 miles east, District 3, in town

Beaubassin

End of Acadian odyssey from Beaubassin, Nova Scotia, via St. James and Atchafalaya swamps, to the Attakapas prairies. Here Louis Pierre Arceneaux, prototype of Longfellow's Gabriel, established his ranch in 1765.

CARMEL (DeSoto Parish)
District 4, in town
Pierre Boitt Lafitte

Grave of Pierre Boitt Lafitte, son of pirate Pierre Lafitte, hero in defense of New Orleans against British in 1815. He owned an 11,963-acre grant. A community, lake, and river were named for him.

CARVILLE (Iberville Parish)
District 61, in front of
U.S. Public Health Service Hospital
Indian Camp Plantation

The plantation home, built in the 1850s, became the site of the Louisiana State Leprosarium in 1894. The U.S. Public Health Service acquired it in 1921. It is now known as the National Hansen's Disease Center.

CASTOR (Bienville Parish)
In town
Site of King's Salt Works—located ¼ mile west

Alfred Pickney King began salt operations at this site in the 1840s. During the Civil War, King's Salt Works increased production to supply much needed salt to the Confederacy.

CENTERVILLE (Livingston Parish)
District 62, junction of SH 42
and Doyle Parish Rd.
Centerville, Louisiana

Locally known by above name, although the post office was named Springville. Served as parish seat, 1881 to 1941. Site of first electrocution in the state in 1941. Van Buren, the first parish seat, 1832–35, was on east bank.

CHACHAHOULA (Terrebonne Parish)
SH 40, District 2, in town
Old Cattle Trail

Route led from Mexico to the Mississippi River at Vacherie. One segment, Bull Run Road, starting at Central, ended at Chachahoula. The trail continued West along ridges to Gibson, Morgan City, the Teche lands, on to el Camino Real during latter French and early Spanish period.

CHALMETTE (St. Bernard Parish)　　　*SH 39, District 2, in town*

The Chalmette Plantations

Scene of the Battle of New Orleans Dec. 1814–Jan. 1815. Battle raged on lands of Ignace de Lino de Chalmette, Antoine Bienvenue, and Denis de la Ronde. British camps on lands of Jacques de Villere and Pierre Lacoste; hospital on Jumonville de Villiers. Jackson Defense Line on Edmond Macarty place.

CHALMETTE (St. Bernard Parish)　　　*SH 39, District 2, in town*

de la Ronde House

The de la Ronde House, built in 1805 by Pierre Denis de la Ronde on Versailles Plantation. House was used as a hospital by the British under Sir Edward Pakenham during the Battle of New Orleans January 1815.

CHALMETTE (St. Bernard Parish)　　　*District 2, in town*

Hopedate Sugar Mill

Here at La Chincha, owned by Pierre Ruiz, are the remains of a steam engine sugar mill evaporator put in by Edgar Ruiz in November 1870, the last device of its kind in St. Bernard Parish, a relic of a bygone era.

CHALMETTE (St. Bernard Parish)　　　*SH 39, District 2,*
St. Bernard Parish Library

Lacoste Plantation

Ursuline Nuns' property, 1727; sold to Gui Soniat Dufossat circa 1778; sold by Dufossat Family to Pierre Lacoste, 1796. Seized by British force, Dec., 1714; U.S. forces under Gen. John Coffee routed British in counterattack. Became Villere property in 1856.

CHENEYVILLE (Rapides Parish)　　　*Parish Road 14,*
District 8, near town

Trinity Episcopal Church

Gothic Revival church built of handmade brick in 1860 and designed with separate gallery for slaves. Consecrated by Bishop Leonides Polk in 1861.

Original congregation included several prominent planters of the surrounding area.

Sponsored by Trinity Episcopal Church.

CLARENCE (Natchitoches Parish) *US 71, District 8, in town*

The Natchez Trace
Harrisonburgh Road

This historic road was a vital link between the Natchez Trace and the old Spanish El Camino Real. Over it passed the founding and colonizing pioneers who paved the way for the settlement and development of Western Louisiana and Eastern Texas.

CLARENCE (Natchitoches Parish) *US 71/84, District 8, in town*

Natchitoches

Oldest settlement in the Louisiana Purchase, 7 miles west. Steeped in romance and tradition, here you will find the true flavor of the Old South amid scenes of great beauty of Cane River.

CLAYTON (Concordia Parish) *District 58, in town*

Probable Site of Aminoya

Within this site is the probable site of the prehistoric city of Aminoya. After attempting to reach Mexico, Luis de Moscoso, de Soto's successor, led his men back here. From here they started down the Mississippi River to the Gulf of Mexico in brigantines they had built.

CLINTON (East Feliciana Parish) *District 61, in town*

Clinton Courthouse

This courthouse, built in 1840, is one of the architectural treasures of the state. The present building replaced a wooden courthouse that dated from 1825–26, which was burned in March 1839. This is one of the oldest courthouses in Louisiana which is still in daily use.

CLINTON (East Feliciana Parish) *District 61, in town*

Lawyer's Row

Constructed c. 1840–1865. Outstanding group of early 19th century Classical style offices. Early occupants were noted for their contributions to the political and judicial history of the area and the state.

CLINTON (East Feliciana Parish) *District 61, in front of St. Andrew's Church*

St. Andrew's Episcopal Church

First Episcopal services in Clinton conducted in 1842 by Rev. William B. Lacey, president of College of Louisiana at Jackson. Parish organized in 1852. Rev. Frederick Dean was first resident priest. Present church dates from 1871.

CLINTON (East Feliciana Parish) *District 61, in town*

Sugartown

Situated in the disputed area once claimed by Spain and the U.S., called "NO MAN'S LAND"; the site of Sugartown Academy, a pioneer educational institution in southwestern Louisiana. The school was of sufficient importance in 1875 to be listed by the La. Education Dept.

CLOUTIERVILLE (Natchitoches Parish) *District 8, at Bayou Folk Museum*

Bayou Folk Museum

Home of Kate Chopin 1880–1883, reknown writer of Creole Short Stories set in famed Cane River Country. Best known for "Bayou Folk" and "A Night in Acadie." Home built in early 1800s by Alexis Cloutier on Spanish Land Grant #1701.

CLOUTIERVILLE (Natchitoches Parish) *SH 1,*
2½ miles south, District 8

Sang Pour Sang Hill

Site of the defeat of the Natchez Indians in 1732 by French troops and their Indian allies, after the Natchez had attacked Fort St. Jean Baptiste de Natchitoches. 2½ miles south.

COATES BLUFF (Caddo Parish)

Coates Bluff

Two blocks east is site of Coates Bluff settlement and homes of early area settlers Larkin Edwards, c. 1803, James Coates, c. 1817, and John McLeod, c. 1835. The first local post office was located here in April, 1838.
Sponsored by Caddo Magnet High School History Club.

COCOVILLE (Avoyelles Parish) *District 8, in town,*
between Marksville and Mansura

Presentation Academy

Site of first Catholic school in Avoyelles Parish—1855. Founded by Daughters of the Cross of Treguier, France, under Mother Mary Hyacinth Le Conniat on request of Bishop Martin Battle of Mansura, May 16, 1864, began on Convent Grounds.

COLFAX (Grant Parish) *SH 8, District 58, in town*

Colfax Riot

On this site occurred the Colfax Riot in which three white men and 150 Negroes were slain. This event on April 13, 1873, marked the end of carpet-bag misrule in the South.

COLUMBIA (Caldwell Parish) *District 58, in front of*
First United Methodist Church

First United Methodist Church

Methodists have worshipped in a building on this site since before 1840. Circuit riders served congregation until 1847, when first pastor appointed.

Present building completed in 1911 from plans brought from Europe by a church member.

Paid for by a church member.

COLUMBIA (Ouachita Parish) *US 165, District 5, in town*

Ouachita River Steamboat Era
1819–1927

Columbia, Louisiana—established 1827. Only settlement between Monroe and Black River towns, noted for its port and steamboat captains.

CONVENT (St. James Parish) *SH 44, District 2, in town*

Convent

Settled in 1722–1739 as Baron, now parish seat St. James Parish. St. Michael's Church 1809. Site of St. Michael's Convent, Order of the Sacred Heart 1825–1932. Site of Jefferson College 1831–1931.

CONVENT (St. James Parish) *River Road, District 61*

Judge Poche Plantation House

Felix Pierre Poche, Civil War diarist, Democratic party leader, prominent jurist, and one of founders of American Bar Association, built this Victorian Renaissance Revival style plantation house with unusual front dormer c. 1870.

CONVENT (St. James Parish) *River Road, District 61,*
in front of Malarcher House, near town

Malarcher House Marker

This house is near site of mansion of Le Chevalier Louis Malarcher (1754–1841), political refugee of French Revolution who became an influential citizen of St. James Parish. Original mansion destroyed in 1890 by levee break which created Nita Crevasse ¼ mile north. In 1891, Willy Malarcher, grandson of the Chevalier, built present house. Some features, however, date from earlier period.

Sponsored by Convent Chemical Corporation.

CONVENT (St. James Parish) *River Road, District 2,*
between Burnside and Gramercy

Tezcuco Plantation

Built in 1855 by Benjamin F. Tureaud, kinsman of Bringier family. Constructed of homemade red brick and Louisiana cypress. Purchased in 1888 by Dr. Julian T. Bringier. Retained by relatives until 1940s.

CONVENT (St. James Parish) *SH 44 (River Road), District 2*

Uncle Sam Plantation

First named Constancia (1812), Uncle Sam was one of Louisiana's great sugar plantations. Erected by owner Samuel P. A. Fagot between 1837–1843, the mansion and its many side buildings dominated this site until demolished during move of river levee in 1940.

CONVENT (St. James Parish) *District 2, near town*

White Hall Plantation (La Maison Blanche)

Spanish Colonial plantation home, erected in the 1790s. Famous guests said to have visited La Maison Blanche include the duc d'Orleans, later King Louis Philippe of France, and General Andrew "Old Hickory" Jackson. General W. C. C. Claiborne was a guest in 1806. Noted Revolutionary War Colonel Wade Hampton purchased the property in 1825. White Hall changed hands several times before it burned about 1850.

COTTONPORT (Avoyelles Parish) *In town*

The Historic Oaks of Cottonport

The history of Cottonport began about 1823 when Joseph Ducote II married Marguerite Bordelon. On the bank of Bayou Rouge he cleared a cane brake, built a house, and planted these oak trees. About 1835 he donated some of his property for a road and a one-room school house. This is considered the first planning effort for the town of Cottonport.
Sponsored by Cottonport Centennial.

COVINGTON (St. Tammany Parish)   *District 62,*
120 N. New Hampshire St.
Christ Episcopal Church

Built 1846 by Jonathan Arthur of London for descendants of English set-
tlers in British West Florida, consecrated by Bishop Leonidas K. Polk,
April 11, 1847, Christ Church is the oldest public building being used in
Covington.

COVINGTON (St. Tammany Parish)   *SH 190, District 62, in town*
Covington

John Wharton Collins donated land and founded Wharton in 1813. Town
was named for his grandfather, John Wharton. Legislature granted charter
March 11, 1816, and changed name to Covington, in honor of Gen. Leonard
A. Covington, war hero of 1812.

CROWLEY (Acadia Parish)   *In town*
Crowley

Founded 1886 and soon emerged as center of state's rice industry. Historic
district listed on National Register of Historic Places. Significant for its
impressive c. 1890 – c. 1930 commercial area and its superb Victorian residences.

CROWLEY (Acadia Parish)   *District 3, in town, Rice Festival*
Salmon Lusk Wright
1852–1929

Developed at this site the world's best seed rice which revived that industry by insuring wider markets. His varieties that are used today for breeding
purposes are Blue Rose, Louisiana Pearl, Early Prolific Edith, and Lady
Wright.

DARROW (Ascension Parish)   *SH 30 (River Road), District 61*

Ashland

Plantation home of Duncan Farrar Kenner, 1813–1887; statesman, lawyer, planter, and Confederate minister to France and England in 1864. Home also known as Belle Helene.

DENHAM SPRINGS (Livingston Parish)   *District 62, in town*

Denham Springs

Mineral spring area near here owned by William Denham 1829–1855. Hotel near the springs built prior to the Civil War. Hill's Springs post office renamed Denham Springs in 1898. The village was incorporated in 1903.

DENHAM SPRINGS (Livingston Parish)   *District 62, SH 16, six miles south*

Hebron Baptist Church

Oldest in Livingston Parish. Organized April 1837. First church was log cabin 3 miles south of here. Frame church built at this site in 1859 on 4 acres of land. 1918 and 1955 larger churches built. Thomas M. Bond first pastor.

DEQUINCY (Calcasieu Parish)   *In front of church, in town*

All Saints Episcopal Church

Built in 1855 in Patterson, La. and originally known as Holy Trinity. Moved to present location in 1942. Listed on National Register of Historic Places because of its superior Gothic Revival architecture.

DEQUINCY (Calcasieu Parish)   *In front of depot, in town*

Kansas City Southern Depot

Built in 1923, the depot is an outstanding example of Mission Revival architecture, and is one of the most architecturally significant railroad depots in the state. Listed on National Register of Historic Places.

DES ALLEMANDS (St. Charles Parish)   *US 90, District 2, in town*
Battle of Des Allemands

Le district des Allemands, settled by Germans about 1720, the scene of numerous skirmishes between Confederate guerillas and Union forces, 1862–1863. Most famous skirmish resulted in capture of an entire detachment of Union soldiers on September 4, 1862.

DESTREHAN (St. Charles Parish)   *9999 River Road, District 2*
Destrehan Manor House

Constructed 1789–1790 for Robert de Logny. Inherited by Jean Noel d'Estrehan 1800. Bought from heirs of Pierre A. Rost in 1914 by Mexican Petroleum Co. Donated 1972 to River Road Historical Society by American Oil Co.

DESTREHAN (Jefferson Parish)   *SH 48, District 2, in town*
St. Charles Borromeo "Little Red Church"

First constructed of logs about 1740. Burned and rebuilt, 1806. Famous riverboat landmark, twenty-five miles from New Orleans where boat captains traditionally paid off their crews. Again burned and rebuilt about 1921.

DONALDSONVILLE (Ascension Parish)   *District 61, in town*
Ascension Catholic Church

This church founded August 15, 1772, by Father Angel de Revillagodos on orders of King Charles III of Spain. Cornerstone of present church laid June 1876 by Bishop Elder of Natchez and April 14, 1896, dedicated by Archbishop Janssens of New Orleans.

DONALDSONVILLE (Ascension Parish)   *SH 404, District 61, in town*
Donaldsonville—Second Acadian Coast

Town founded by William Donaldsonville, 1806, on farm of Pierre Landry. Began as trading post about 1750. Home of Governor Frances T. Nicholls, of Dr. F. W. Prevost, who performed first Caesarian section, 1824. Parish seat of Ascension. Capital of Louisiana Jan. 1830 to Jan. 1831.

DONALDSONVILLE (Ascension Parish)   *District 61, in town*

Donaldsonville

Made capital of Louisiana in 1830; Legislature met from January 4 to March 16 and reconvened in 1831. In 1848 the old State House, located across from this site, was razed, and its bricks used to prevent wave-wash at the bayou's mouth.

DONALDSONVILLE (Ascension Parish)   *US 61, District 61, in town*

First Missionary Martyr

Jean Francois Buisson De St. Cosme of Quebec Seminary, Canada. First American-born priest killed in this country and in Louisiana near this site by Indians, 1706.

DONALDSONVILLE (Ascension Parish)   *SH 1, District 2, in town*

Francis T. Nicholls
1834–1912

On this site directly across from this marker Francis T. Nicholls—Confederate General, Governor, and Chief Justice of the State Supreme Court—was born and reared.

DONALDSONVILLE (Ascension Parish)   *SH 1, District 61,*
                                                              in front of St. Emma

St. Emma Plantation

Scene of Civil War skirmish in fall of 1862. C. 1850 Greek Revival plantation house owned 1854–1869 by Charles A. Kock, a prominent sugar planter. Listed on National Register of Historic Places in 1980.

DOYLINE (Webster Parish)   *SH 164/165, District 4, in town*

Lake Bistineau

Steamboat channel created by Red River log jam 1793. Twelve miles south is Lake Bistineau State Park, near a salt dome where salt was manufactured by some 1,500 people during the War Between the States blockade.

DUBACH (Lincoln Parish) *US 167, south of town*
Unionville General Store

Originally established in 1853 overlooking Bayou D'Arbonne. In this location since 1888, when present building constructed. This country store has been a community focal point. Unionville is the home of the Colvin family reunion.

Sponsored by the Department of Culture, Recreation, and Tourism.

EARL WILLIAMSON PARK (Caddo Parish) *SH 1, District 4, just south of Oil City*
Huddie "Leadbelly" Ledbetter

Blues singer from Mooringsport, La. (1888–1949). He played 12-string guitar on Shreveport's Fannin St., sang his way out of prison, and became a folk hero with songs like "Goodnight Irene," "Bourgeois Blues," and "Midnight Special."

EDGARD (St. John the Baptist Parish) *SH 18, District 2, in town*
St. John the Baptist Catholic Church
1770

From which civil parish was named. First church on second German Coast when Louisiana was colony of Spain. Served west and east banks of river until 1864. Old cemetery contains grave of wife of Gen. P. G. T. Beauregard and John Slidell family tomb.

ELTON (Jefferson Davis Parish) *US 190, District 7, in town*
Coushatta Indians

Three miles north is tribe that migrated, 1795, to Louisiana from Alabama. Name means "White Reedbrake" and Coushatta, town in Red River Parish, named for them. Noted for basket handicraft.

EPPS (West Carroll Parish) *SH 17, District 5, in town*
Poverty Point

About 1000 B.C. a notable prehistoric culture flourished on this Indian site in the lower Mississippi Valley. The octagonal village terraces, the immense mounds, and the stone artifacts were unique for early agricultural, prepottery people.

ERWINVILLE (Pointe Coupee Parish)   *SH 190, District 61, near town*
Randall Oak

On False River, 11.5 miles north, where James Randall wrote "Maryland My Maryland." And 8 miles north is Parlange Plantation home, containing many early Louisiana relics.

EUNICE (St. Landry Parish)   *District 03, in front of Eunice Railroad Depot*
City of Eunice

On this site C. C. Duson drove a stake and said: "On this spot I will build a town and name it for my wife, Eunice." An auction of lots was held here to start the town, Sept. 12, 1894. Depot listed on National Register of Historic Places.
Sponsored by Matt Vernon.

EVERGREEN (Avoyelles Parish)   *SH 361*
Evergreen

Site of Evergreen Home Institute (1856); Henry Clay Kemper, 1st headmaster. Later became Evergreen College; then Evergreen High School in 1904. These schools had a noteworthy influence on education in Avoyelles and Louisiana.

FERRIDAY (Concordia Parish)   *US 65/84, District 58, in town*
Hernando de Soto

Intrepid Spanish conquistador who traversed half of North America, died near here at the Indian Village of Guahoya, May 21, 1542. He was buried in the Mississippi River, which he discovered.

FISHER (Sabine Parish)   *District 8, in town*

Village of Fisher

Named for Oliver Williams Fisher, the village was built 1899–1901 by Louisiana Long Leaf Lumber Company. It remained a company-owned sawmill town until it was sold to Boise Cascade Corporation in 1966.

FORT POLK (Vernon Parish)   *SH 10, near town,*
                                              at CCC Commemorative Area

Civilian Conservation Corps

CCC planted these slash pine in 1939 in Kisatchie National Forest. CCC reforestation and construction of dams, roads, fire towers and recreation areas (1933–42) contributed to a rebirth in Vernon Parish's forest industry.

FORTS BUHLOW AND RANDOLPH (Rapides Parish)   *US 165,*
                                            near Central Louisiana
                                                     State Hospital

Fort Buhlow and Fort Randolph

Fort Buhlow and Fort Randolph were earthwork/moat fortifications constructed beginning October 1864, by Confederate forces anticipating a repetition of Union Gen. Nathaniel Banks' summer 1864 Red River Expedition. Construction, completed by March 1865, was under the command of Capt. C. M. Randolph and supervised by a Military Engineer, Lt. A. Buhlow, for whom the forts are named. The work was performed by about 1,500 soldiers and civilian workers and 500 black slaves. A third and larger fort, planned for the Alexandria side of the river, was never built. There was a Confederate troop build-up in the Alexandria area in March 1865, and the Confederate ironclad *Missouri* was anchored in the river opposite Fort Randolph, but the anticipated attack never came and no fighting ever took place. On May 26th, Gen. Simon Buckner surrendered all Confederate forces in the Trans-Mississippi area, and Union forces under Gen. Phillip Sheridan occupied Buhlow and Randolph on June 2, 1865. Fort Buhlow is now a State Park. Fort Buhlow is located approximately 60 yards upstream (north) of the O.K. Allen Bridge on U.S. Highway 71. Fort Randolph is located approximately 600 yards downstream (South) from the bridge.

Sponsored by T.O. Moore Chapter, United Daughters of the Confederacy.

FRANKLIN (St. Mary Parish)   *US 90, District 3, in town*
Alexander Porter

Born Donegal County, Ireland June 24, 1785; died Jan. 13, 1844. Early political leader and statesman. Constitutional Convention (1811–1812). Louisiana Legislature (1816–1817). Louisiana Supreme Court (1821–1833). U.S. Senate (1833–1844). Built Oaklawn Manor, 1837; Close friend, Henry Clay, visited him there in 1842.

FRANKLIN (St. Mary Parish)   *US 90, District 3, in town*
Battle of Franklin

Gen. Richard Taylor's 1,600-man Confederate Army fought severe delaying battle here against 4,000 Federals under Gen. Cuvier Grover April 14, 1863, before retreating toward Opelousas.

FRANKLIN (St. Mary Parish)   *District 3, on courthouse grounds*
Charles Austin O'Neill

Franklin native, Chief Justice CHARLES A. O'NEILL, 1869–1951. On Louisiana Supreme Court bench, 1914–1949. Stamped as one of the state's immortals for his contributions to law in the United States and in the cause of justice and freedom.

FRANKLIN (St. Mary Parish)   *US 90, District 3, in town*
Donelson Caffery
1835–1906

Site of home of Donelson Caffery, courageous soldier of the Confederacy; distinguished lawyer and sugar planter of St. Mary Parish; able and uncompromising member of United States Senate (1892–1901); a most influential figure in the history of Louisiana.

FRANKLIN (St. Mary Parish)   *US 90, District 3, in town*
Franklin

Named for Benjamin Franklin in 1800 by founder Alexander "Guinea" Lewis, town became St. Mary Parish seat in 1811, was incorporated in 1830, served as Teche Country's port of entry and trade center until coming of rail-road in 1870s.

FRANKLIN (St. Mary Parish)   *District 3, in Courthouse Square*
Jared Young Sanders
1869–1944

Governor of Louisiana, 1908–1912. Born Avoca Plantation near Morgan City. Law firm located near Franklin courthouse. Served in Louisiana Legislature and U.S. Congress from Franklin.

FRANKLIN (St. Mary Parish)   *US 90, District 3, in town*
Murphy James Foster
1849–1921

Home of Murphy J. Foster, prominent St. Mary Parish plantation owner and lawyer of the reconstruction period who served the people of Louisiana with honor and distinction as: Louisiana State Senator (1880–1892), Thirty-first Governor (1892–1900), United States Senator (1901–1912).

FRANKLINTON (Washington Parish)   *District 62, in town*
First Church

One half mile west is the site of the Half Moon Bluff Baptist Church, organized in 1812, the first Protestant church in Louisiana outside of New Orleans.

FRANKLINTON (Washington Parish)   *District 62, in town*
First School Washington Parish
1809–1810

300-odd yards west near spring on John Bankston's creek. Next after establishing homes, children were taught in log cabin by bachelor Matt McCain in summers.

FRANKLINTON (Washington Parish)   *District 62, in town*
Old Choctaw Trail

Only official state road in Washington Parish until 1843. Choctaw Indians cut trail for trade with tribes in Baton Rouge, New Orleans, Biloxi, and Mobile. White man believed to have used trail as early as 1542.

FRANKLINTON (Washington Parish)   *District 62, in town*
Parish Courthouse

Barn 100 feet east marks site of first justice seat for Washington Parish. It served as Courthouse from March 1820, until removed to present site in 1823, with Col. Thomas Warner as presiding judge.

FRENCH SETTLEMENT (Livingston Parish)   *District 62, in town*
French Settlement

"La Cote Francaise." Settled in 1800 via Amite River by French, German, and Italian "emigres." Jovial Creole culture was unique. Cypress sawmills, trapping, shingle making, farms, and steamboat service once thrived here.

FULLERTON (Vernon Parish)   *In town*
Fullerton Mill & Town

Fullerton Recreation Area was the site of the largest pine sawmill West of the Mississippi River. Between 1907–1927, it was a thriving town of 5,000 people. The industrial area had sawmills, alcohol plant, kiln, and machine shop. A nearby trail passes through some of these remains. The living area had parks, waterfalls, shaded avenues, and "modern" conveniences like electricity and inside plumbing. The community also had churches, schools, hotel, hospital, theater, and swimming pool. Fullerton was placed on the National Register of Historic Places in 1986.
Sponsored by USDA Forest Service.

GALVEZ (Ascension Parish)   *SH 42, District 61, in town*
Galveztown

Old Spanish town at junction of Amite River and Bayou Manchac. Settled by Anglo-Americans, 1776–78, seeking Spanish refuge from American Revolution, and by Canary Islanders (Islenos). Named for Spanish Governor Bernardo de Galvez. Town was abandoned by 1810.

GIBSON (Terrebonne Parish)   *In town, in front of church*
Gibson Methodist Episcopal Church

Erected 1849 on land donated by Cornelius and John Wallis. During Civil War church was used as hospital. Entered National Register of Historic Places May 8, 1986.

GOLDONNA (Natchitoches Parish)   *SH 156, District 8, near town*
Drake's Salt Works

First noted by Bienville in 1700, this site is one of the oldest salt wells in Louisiana. First used by the Indians, it provided a major supply of salt for Confederate forces during the War Between the States.

GRAMERCY (Ascension Parish)   *District 61, in town*
Gramercy

Incorporated November, 1947, located partly on Indian-French settlement and trading post site. In 1739 much of this area was sold to Joseph Delille Dupart, a Commissioner of Indian Nations under Bienville. Today area is location of various industries.

GRAND COTEAU (St. Landry Parish)   *District 3, in town*
Grand Coteau

Early and important center of Catholic education. Noted for its Creole architecture. Town developed around Academy of Sacred Heart, founded in 1821, and St. Charles Jesuit College, founded in 1837.

GREENSBURG (St. Helena Parish)   *District 62, in town*
William Kendrick Square

St. Helena Parish Seat moved here 1832. Land for Court House Square donated by William Kendrick 1837. Present building completed 1938 replacing brick structure built 1855. Designated William Kendrick Square by Police Jury.

GRETNA (Jefferson Parish) *District 02, in front of Gretna City Hall*
City of Gretna

Incorporated 20 August 1913. John Ehret, first Mayor. Seat of Jefferson Parish Government since 1884. German settlement laid out in 1836 by Benjamin Buisson for Nicolas Noel Destrehan as VILLAGE OF MECHANIKHAM.

Sponsored by Twilight Gardeners of Gretna in cooperation with Gretna Historical Society.

HAHNVILLE (St. Charles Parish) *SH 18, District 2, in town*
Fashion Plantation

Home General Richard Taylor, son of Zachary Taylor, Louisiana Statesman and member of 1861 Secession Convention. Commanded Louisiana District, 1862–64; defeated Banks at Battle of Mansfield, 1864. Federals plundered home in 1862.

HAHNVILLE (St. Charles Parish) *SH 18, District 2, in town*
Flagville

Named for O. J. Flagg, 1870. Now a part of Hahnville. Letter left here by de Tonti, 1686, with Quinipissa, Chief for LaSalle. Taensa Village, 1713. De Meuve, French Concession, 1718. Site included grant to Joseph Roi de Villere, 1765.

HAMMOND (Tangipahoa Parish) *District 62, in town*
City of Hammond

Railroad came through in 1854. Became a shoemaking center for the Confederacy during the Civil War. Town was planned in the 1860s, and by early twentieth century was known as "Strawberry Capital of America."

HAMMOND (Tangipahoa Parish)   *District 62, in town*
Grace Memorial Episcopal Church
First service: March 12, 1876, by Bishop Joseph Wilmer, Rev. Herman Duncan first Rector. Land donated by C. E. Cate. Anonymous N.Y. church-woman benefactor. Dedicated 1888 in memory of Mertie A. Cate.

HAMMOND (Tangipahoa Parish)   *District 62, in town, on post office grounds*
Mt. Vernon Walnut
This tree grew from a seed of a walnut tree at George Washington's home at Mt. Vernon. Planted Feb. 22, 1932, by the American Legion Auxiliary and Boy Scouts of Hammond in celebration of Washington's bicentennial. Was transplanted in this location on Feb 22, 1938, by Hammond Garden Club.

HAMMOND (Tangipahoa Parish)   *SH 190, District 62, in town*
Peter Hammond
1798–1870
Under this oak is buried Peter Hammond, of Sweden, who founded Hammond, Louisiana, about 1818. Nearby are the graves of his wife, three daughters, and a favorite slave boy.

HARAHAN (Jefferson Parish)   *Jefferson Hwy., District 2, at Brookhollow Business Park*
Lafreniere Plantation
Part of the concession in 1720 by Governor Bienville to father of Nicholas Chauvin LaFreniere, Attorney-General of Louisiana for the years 1763 until 1769; leader of 1768 revolt against Spanish rulers of Louisiana, and executed October 25, 1769.

HARAHAN (Jefferson Parish)   *SH 48, District 2*
Tchoupitoulas Plantation
Site of plantation acquired in 1808 by Joseph Soniat du Fossat. Visited by Governor William C. C. Claiborne and, legend says, pirateer Jean Lafitte. "Chapitoulas" Indians, whose name means "river people," lived in this area.

HARRISONBURG (Catahoula Parish)   *SH 124/8, District 58, in town*
Fort Beauregard
One half mile west was one of four forts built by Confederates in May, 1863, to prevent the ascent of Federal gunboats on the Ouachita River. It was abandoned 1863, but was reoccupied in 1864.

HARVEY (Jefferson Parish)   *East side of Destrehan Ave.,*
450 feet north of railroad
Harvey Castle Site
Built in 1844, Harvey Castle was the Gothic Revival home of Marie Louise Destrehan and her husband Joseph Hale Harvey. It served as the third courthouse of Jefferson Parish, 1874–84. Located east side of Destrehan Avenue 450 feet north of railroad. Demolished in 1924 to enlarge Harvey Canal and Locks.
Sponsored by Jefferson Historical Society of Louisiana.

HARVEY CANAL (Jefferson Parish)   *District 02, near town*
The Harvey Canal
Originally Destrehan Canal, dug before 1845, connecting Mississippi River to Bayou Barataria. "Submarine Railway" lifted boats over the levee until successful completion of locks in 1907. Became part of Gulf Intra-coastal Waterway in 1924.
Sponsored by the Jefferson Historical Society of Louisiana.

HOLDEN (Livingston Parish)   *District 62, SH 1036, 8 miles northwest*
Macedonia Baptist Church
Organized in 1956. Existing building constructed in 1898. Oldest Baptist church building in Livingston Parish. Drinking water furnished by ground water spring. Surrounding area settled by Anglo-Saxon Protestants in 1800s.

HOMER (Claiborne Parish)   *District 4, on school grounds*
Arizona Academy Site
Donated by Joshua Willis to J. W. Nicholson who organized a private school, 1867–1869. Nicholson later president of L.S.U. School was one of

the leading academies in state. Became public school 1910. T. H. Harris a noted graduate.

HOMER (Claiborne Parish) — *District 4, in Court House Square*
Claiborne Parish Courthouse

Built in 1860, this antebellum building was the point of departure for Confederate troops during the War Between the States. It is one of the finest examples of Southern expression of Greek architectural style.

HOUMA (Terrebonne Parish) — *US 90, district 2, in town*
Isles Dernieres (Last Island)

Over 200 persons were killed when a giant tidal wave hit Last Island, 45 miles south of Houma, on Aug. 10, 1856. The resort was a playground for Southern aristocrats. Fishermen (with boats) call it a Sportsman's Paradise.

HOUMA (Terrebonne Parish) — *District 03, in front of Orange Grove, near town*
Orange Grove

Built c. 1840. Noted for its handsome Greek Revival styling, its briquette-entre-poteaux (bricks set between posts) construction, and its faux bois (false grained) woodwork. Listed in National Register of Historic Places.
Sponsored by owner.

HYMEL (St. James Parish) — *SH 18, District 2, in town*
Cabahanoce Plantation—St. James

House long since claimed by the river was home of Andre Bienvenu Roman (1831–35 and 1839–43), Governor of Louisiana (1845 and 1852), Member Constitutional Convention (1861), Member Secession Convention Member Peace Commission to Washington, D.C. for Confederacy.

HYMEL (St. James Parish) — *SH 18, District 2, in town*
Saint Jacques de Cabahanoce

An organized ecclesiastical parish prior to 1757. The church was then in charge of Fr. Barnabe, a French capuchin and pastor of Saint Charles

(Destrehan), on east bank of river. The registers were kept in French until 1786. The diocese came under Havana, Cuba, in 1771.

INDEPENDENCE (Tangipahoa Parish) *SH 40*
Independence
Known as Uncle Sam when settled in 1830s. Italian families began to arrive in early 1880s. Because of this heritage, the town has come to be known as "Little Italy." Downtown historic district created by city in 1982.

INNIS (Pointe Coupee Parish) *SH 1, District 61, LaCour Plantation*
John Archer Lejeune
Lt. General Lejeune, 1867–1942, was born in Innis; commanded the 2nd Division of the AEF during WWI; became Commandant of USMC; was superintendent of VMI from 1929 to 1937.

JACKSON (East Feliciana Parish) *SH 10, District 61*
East Louisiana State Hospital
400 yrds. south of here stands the main building of East Louisiana State Hospital, built 1847–54 as the state's first permanent facility for the care of the mentally ill. One of the finest examples of Greek Revival style in La.
Sponsored by East Louisiana State Hospital Auxiliary.

JACKSON (East Feliciana Parish) *District 61, in town*
Feliciana Courthouse
1816–1824
Jackson became the seat of justice for Feliciana Parish by Act of Legislature, Jan. 1815. Public town square donated by James Ficklin and John Horton. In active use until parish divided into East and West Feliciana in February 1824.

JACKSON (East Feliciana Parish) *District 61, in town*
Jackson
Founded as seat of justice for Feliciana Parish, 1815. College of Louisiana founded here, 1825. Became Centenary College, 1845. State insane asylum founded here, 1847. Historic district on National Register of Historic Places.

JANESVILLE (West Carroll Parish)   *SH 586, 4.4 miles from*
                                                SH 17, District 5

Site of Janesville

Frank Janes came here c. 1908, followed by John Janes and other Croatians. The Frank Janes Company produced and exported barrel staves for use in French claret production. Janesville flourished until company disbanded in 1928.

JEANERETTE (Iberia Parish)   *District 3, in town,*
                                                north side of Bayou Teche

Bayside Plantation

This house was built in 1850 by Francis D. Richardson on Bayou Teche in Greek Revival style of the period. Richardson, a classmate and friend of Edgar Allan Poe, purchased the land for a sugar plantation. Named Bayside because of dense growth of bay trees nearby.

JEANERETTE (Iberia Parish)   *US 90, District 3, in town*

Beau Pre—Circa 1828

This home, originally known as Pine Grove, was bought in 1830 by John W. Jeanerette, the first postmaster between New Iberia and Charenton, and for whom Jeanerette is named. This historic home escaped the destruction of military operations in the area during the Civil War.

JEANERETTE (Iberia Parish)   *District 3, in town*

Nicolas Provot—"The Father of Jeanerette"

Buried here September 12, 1816. One of this area's first landowners. Town of Jeanerette grew up on site of his plantation. His descendants have been prominent in local history.

JEFFERSON (Jefferson Parish)   *5200–5300 block, Jefferson Hwy.*

Site of Wedell-Williams Airport

During 1930–42 this airport operated passenger, charter, and mail service and a flying school. The company of James R. Wedell and Harry P. Williams designed, built, and flew some of the fastest planes in the world. Wedell set a world speed record in 1933. By 1936 both had died in air crashes. The routes were sold to Eastern Airlines. During WWII this site became part of the U.S. Army Camp Plauche.

Sponsored by the Jefferson Historical Society of Louisiana.

JEFFERSON PARISH (Jefferson Parish)   *District 2, located at*
four entry points to the Parish

Jefferson Parish

On Feb. 11, 1825, Governor Henry S. Johnson signed legislation creating the Parish of Jefferson out of the Third Senatorial District. It is named for President Thomas Jefferson, who died the following year, July 4.

Sponsored by the Jefferson Parish Historical Commission.

JEFFERSON ISLAND (Vermilion Parish)   *District 3, in town*

Jefferson Island

Once known as Orange Island, purchased after the Civil War by Joseph Jefferson (1829 to 1905), world famous actor and artist. Home designed and built about 1870.

JENNINGS (Jefferson Davis Parish)   *SH 90, District 7, in town*

First Oil Well

Jennings Oil Company Number 1, Jules Clement, was completed at Evangeline, 5 miles northeast, Sept. 21, 1901, by W. Scott Heywood and Associates. This was the start of the vital Louisiana Oil and Gas Industry.

JENNINGS (Jefferson Davis Parish)   *SH 90, District 7, in town*

First Refinery

Directly north stands one of the original buildings which housed Louisiana's first oil refinery. Built in 1903, it marked the start of Louisiana's petrochemical industry.

JONESVILLE (Catahoula Parish) *US 84, District 58, in town*

Ancient Anilco

The capital of a populous Indian Province, and site of the Great Mound, 80 feet high. Hernando de Soto arrived here March 29, 1542, and he later returned to fight his last battle here.

KEACHIE (DeSoto Parish) *In town*

Confederate Cemetery

Within this enclosure are the remains of over 100 Confederate soldiers. Following the Battle of Mansfield, many were infirmed at old Keachie College, where a morgue was established on the second floor of the main building.

Sponsored by Gen. Richard Taylor Camp #1308, Sons of Confederate Veterans, and Betty Youree Chapter #425, Children of the Confederacy.

KENNER (Jefferson Parish) *District 2, in town*

Cannes Brulees (Burnt Canes)

Zone between les Chapitoulas and the Demeuves Concession. Five leagues above New Orleans along the Mississippi River. From 1708–1819, this name was in use under French, Spanish, and American rule. Site of present day Kenner.

Sponsored by the Jefferson Historical Society of Louisiana.

KENNER (Jefferson Parish) *In town*

Kenner Town Hall

The hub of Kenner city government was built in 1926 to house the town hall, jail, and courthouse. In 1956, city hall moved. The jail and courthouse relocated in 1970. Today it houses the Kenner Office of Tourism.

Sponsored by the city of Kenner.

KENNER (St. Charles Parish) *In front of house near town*

Labranche Plantation Dependency

This late eighteenth–early nineteenth century Creole house is of statewide significance because of its exceptional Federal woodwork and its rarity as a plantation dependency. Listed on National Register of Historic Places.

KENNER (Jefferson Parish) *District 2, in town at Jefferson Hwy. and Suave*

La Providence

Concession 1720s–1730s on the Chim de la Metairie. Birthplace Jacques Phillippe Roi de Villere 1761–1830, first native born Governor of Louisiana 1816–1820.

KENTWOOD (Tangipahoa Parish) *US 51, District 62, in town*

Roncal

Site of Civil War home of Charles Etienne Arthur Gayarre, Louisiana historian, lawyer, judge, legislator, and Secretary of State 1846–1853. Grandson of Etienne de Bore.

KILLONA (St. Charles Parish) *District 2, in town*

Les Allemands

German immigrants, led by Karl D'Arensbourg, joined other Germans from John Law's Arkansas concession to settle here in 1722. Chapel erected by 1724. These industrious German farmers saved New Orleans from famine.
Sponsored by German-Acadian Coast Historical & Genealogical Society.

KINDER (Allen Parish) *In town*

Kinder, Louisiana

Named for James A. Kinder, who received a homestead certificate for land in 1892. Kansas City, Watkins, and Gulf Railway arrived in 1890. Kinder was incorporated as a village in 1903. Patrick E. Moore served as first mayor.
Sponsored by Town of Kinder.

LABADIEVILLE (Assumption Parish) *SH 1, District 2, near town*

White Home

South 8 miles on Bayou Lafourche is birthplace of Edward Douglass White, Louisiana's Confederate Soldier, Statesman, Journalist, and Chief Justice of U.S. Supreme Court.

LACOMBE (St. Tammany Parish)   *District 62, in town*
Abbe Adrien E. Rouquette

Abbe Rouquette (1813–1887), poet and priest, lived as missionary among Choctaw Indians in region of Bayou Lacombe from 1859 till his death. The Choctaws called him "Chata Ima," meaning "like a Choctaw."

Abbe Adrien E. Rouquette

Abbe Rouquette (1813–1887), poete et pretre, vecut comme un missionaire entre les Indiens Choctaws de la region Bayou Lacombe de 1859 jusqu 'a sa mort. Les Choctaws l'appelerent "Chata Ima" qui est "comme un Choctaw."
Sponsored by Bayou Lacombe Bicentennial Community.

LACOUR (Pointe Coupee Parish)   *SH 419, District 61, near town*
LaCour Store

Built circa 1870 by Ovide LaCour. Outstanding example of a plantation store. Owned and operated by LaCour and his descendants until 1975. Entered into National Register of Historic Places in 1979.

LACOUR (Pointe Coupee Parish)   *SH 419, District 61, near town*
Old Hickory

Built circa 1820 by the Zenon Ledoux family. Excellent example of a Creole raised plantation house. Ovide LaCour owned this house and the nearby LaCour Store. Entered into National Register of Historic Places in 1979.

LAFAYETTE (Lafayette Parish)   *US 90, District 3, in town*
The Cathedral of St. John the Evangelist

First Church in Lafayette Parish was "l'Eglise St. Jean du Vermilion." Built on a gift of this site by Jean Mouton, 1821. In 1824 he donated land for a court house and founded Vermilionville (Lafayette).

LAFAYETTE (Lafayette Parish)   *District 3, on Lafayette St.*
Lafayette Museum

Established 1954 by Les Vingt-Quatre. Home of Louisiana's first Democratic Governor Alexandre Mouton (1804–1882). Built prior to 1836.

LAFAYETTE (Lafayette Parish)
District 3, in town
General Alfred Mouton

1829–1864. Confederate brigadier general from Lafayette who served in Shiloh, Lafourche, Teche, and Red River campaigns. Killed at Mansfield, leading Confederacy to its most important military victory west of the Mississippi.

Le General Alfred Mouton

1829–1864. General sudiste de Lafayette qui participa aux campagnes de Shiloh, Lafourche, Teche et Riviere Rouge. Tue a Mansfield en commandant les forces sudistes a leur victoire militaire la plus importante a l'ouest du Mississippi.

Sponsored by Alfred Mouton Chapter, United Daughters of the Confederacy.

LAFAYETTE (Lafayette Parish)
District 3, at Natural History Museum
Pierre Dugat Home Site

In 1776 Pierre Dugat received a Spanish land grant for this site, which became his plantation. Indian artifacts found on this site date from 3000 B.C. to about the eighteenth century.

LAKE CHARLES (Calcasieu Parish)
US 90, District 7, in town
Lake Charles

Chief city of Calcasieu Parish. Here buccaneer Lafitte delivered stolen Negro slaves to James Bowie and other planters. "Calcasieu" is Indian dialect for "Crying Eagle," war chief of the Atakapa.

LAKE CHARLES (Calcasieu Parish)
US 171, District 7
Perkins Ferry

In the 1820s about two miles from here on Calcasieu River, Rees Perkins operated one of the first ferries in this parish; a popular cattle crossing en route from Mexico and Texas to the Teche lands and New Orleans.

LAKE PONTCHARTRAIN (Orleans Parish) *District 2, St. Bernard and Lakeshore Ave.*

Lake Pontchartrain

Traveled on by Iberville, 1699, and named for the French Minister of Marine. Indians called it Okwa-ta, wide water. First port of embarkation was at the site where Bayou St. John flows from this lake. It was the first water travel route to the City of New Orleans.

LAKE PROVIDENCE (East Carroll Parish) *US 65, District 65*

Grant's Canal

In early 1863 Federal General U.S. Grant dug a canal here connecting the Mississippi River and Lake Providence. This attempt to use bayous and rivers to bypass Vicksburg failed.

LAKE PROVIDENCE (East Carroll Parish) *District 65, in town*

Soldiers' Rest

In early 1863, Union troops commanded by Gen. U.S. Grant dug a canal connecting the Mississippi River and Lake Providence. They camped in an area known as "Soldiers' Rest," which provided a temporary home.

LAKELAND (Pointe Coupee Parish) *SH 415, District 61, in town*

False River

Upper end of "Fause Riviere," old Mississippi River Bed. Resulted when the river followed the narrow stream over a neck of land (Pointe Coupee). Used in 1699 by Iberville and party to shorten their route up river. Nearby, Fort St. Joseph est'b c. 1718; St. Francis church, 1738.

LAKELAND (Pointe Coupee Parish) *SH 415, District 61*

Pointe Coupee

Narrow stream o'er portage widened by Iberville and Bienville, 1699. Shortly after 1700 Mississippi River had formed "point cut off," a crescent shaped land, "Pointe Coupee."

LAPLACE (St. John the Baptist Parish)   *SH 61, District 62,*
on highway at site of crevasse

Bonnet Carre Crevasse

In 1871 on this bonnet-shaped curve of the Mississippi River a disastrous break in the levee cut a wide channel to Lake Pontchartrain. Crevasse closed in 1883. Bonnet Carre Spillway completed in 1932.
Sponsored by LaPlace Centennial Committee.

LAPLACE (St. John the Baptist Parish)   *District 62, in front of*
courthouse annex

LaPlace

Town of LaPlace named when a railroad stop was established on the Bazile LaPlace plantation in 1883. Post office followed in 1887. It was first named Eugenia, then renamed LaPlace in 1892.
Sponsored by L'Observateur.

LAPLACE (St. John the Baptist Parish)   *SH 44, District 62*

A. Montz

Armand Montz, Sr., 1887–1968. Built ice and packing plant in 1914; remodeled in 1930s. Packed and shipped vegetables to various parts of U.S. Frozen food industry pioneer. His plant was important factor in local economy.

LAPLACE (St. John the Baptist Parish)   *District 62, intersection of*
US 51 and Airline Hwy.

Woodland Plantation

Acquired in 1793 and 1808 by Manuel Andry, a commandant of the German Coast. Major 1811 slave uprising organized here. Ory Bros. and A. Lasseigne were last owners of plantation. Its subdivision in 1923 spurred growth of LaPlace.
Sponsored by Woodland Planting and Manufacturing Co.

LEESVILLE (Vernon Parish) *US 171, District 8, near town*
Holly Grove Methodist Church

Methodist services in this area began in 1826. This church, located one mile west, was organized in 1835 by Reverend James Ford, one of the circuit riders who served it. The present buildings date from 1894 and 1977.
Sponsored by Holly Grove Methodist Church.

LEESVILLE (Vernon Parish) *District 8, in town*
Sgt. Abe Allen
1896–1941

Only soldier from Louisiana to serve under General John J. Pershing's "One Hundred Heroes" in World War I Company B, 28th Infantry. Received Distinguished Service Cross and the Distinguished Service Medal.

LINWOOD (East Feliciana Parish) *SH 964, District 61, at head of graveled road leading to Linwood*
Linwood

1 mile SW. Built c. 1848 by Albert G. Carter. A portion of Sarah Morgan Dawson's *A Confederate Girl's Diary* was written here. Bombardment of Port Hudson and other events at Linwood are described in this important Civil War source.

LIVINGSTON (Livingston Parish) *District 62, Albany-Springfield exit off I-12*
Hungarian Settlement

Known as Arpadhon, area is site of largest rural Hungarian settlement in U.S. Settlers attracted here in 1896 by Charles Brakenridge lumber mill. People bought cut-over timber land to farm and raise strawberries.

LIVINGSTON (Livingston Parish) *District 62, in town*
Livingston Parish

Created by legislature 1832. Named for Edward Livingston. Courthouse sites include: Van Buren (1832–1835), Springfield (1835–1872), Port Vincent (1872–1881), Centerville (1881–1941), Livingston (1941–present).

LOGANSPORT (DeSoto Parish)   *LA 764/Texas 31, District 58, near town*

International Boundary Marker

Located 170 feet north of here is original granite block 10′ x 9″ which marked United States-Republic of Texas boundary. Dated 1840. Set on April 23, 1841. Only international boundary marker known to exist within continental U.S.

LORANGER (Tangipahoa Parish)   *In town, at the school*

Loranger High School

Original structure, 1912. Present structure, 1930. A community, civic, and educational center. Built under the direction of W. G. Cory, School Board Member—J. F. Corkern, Principal. Marker donated by Loranger High School Alumni Association, organized 1922, and one of the oldest in Louisiana.

LULING (St. Charles Parish)   *District 2, in town*

Home Place

Built in 1790s, this French Colonial raised cottage is of West Indies bousillage construction. Owners included Labranche, Fortier, Gaillaird. Keller family ownership since 1885.

LUTCHER (St. James Parish)   *District 2, in town*

James Mather

Large sugar plantation owned by Mather family until sold in 1879. James Mather, Englishman by birth, came to America in 1777; was active in Indian trade in West Florida area; was fourth mayor of New Orleans serving from 1807–1812. Here, on October 8, 1821, James Mather died.

LUTCHER (St. James Parish)   *District 2, in town*

Lutcher

Established 1891 by H. J. Lutcher, co-owner of Lutcher & Moore Cypress Lumber Co. The town, incorporated in 1912, grew around the sawmill built on the plantation of Pierre Chenet, developer of world-famous Perique tobacco.
Sponsored by the Kraemer family in memory of Clyde Kraemer.

LUTCHER (St. James Parish) *SH 44, District 2, in town*
Vacherie de Grande Pointe

This area, a ridge, extends from Convent through Gramercy and ends at Grand Point in the rear. On this ridge, the world's supply of a unique crop, Perique tobacco, is grown, processed, and shipped. It is also the site of Indian mounds and sugar cane fields.

MADISONVILLE (St. Tammany Parish) *District 62, on Walter Street*
Madisonville

Originally called "Cokie" (from Coquille) because of the abundance of shells in the area. Renamed for Pres. James Madison, c. 1811. Site of Navy Yard in early 1800s. According to legend, Gen. Andrew Jackson, en route to New Orleans in Nov. 1814, stopped here at the home of Gen. David B. Morgan.

MANCHAC (Tangipahoa Parish) *District 62, Manchac Post Office*
Pass Manchac

S. boundary of Tangipahoa Parish. Part of line dividing Isle of Orleans from Florida Parishes. Boundary between Fr. West Florida and Spanish La., 1763–83; Spanish West Florida and French La., 1803; U.S. and Spanish West Florida, 1803–10.

MANDEVILLE (St. Tammany Parish) *District 62, in town*
Fontainebleau

State park, 24 miles west, is the site of the summer plantation home of Bernard de Marigny de Mandeville, colorful and flamboyant figure in early Louisiana history. Sugar mill and plantation ruins remain.

MANDEVILLE (St. Tammany Parish) *District 62, along Lake Ponchartrain*
Mandeville

Named for Pierre Philippe de Marigny de Mandeville, land owner during the late seventeen hundreds. Near this site Bienville met, in 1699, Acolapissas who reported that, two days before, their village had been attacked by two Englishmen and 200 Chickasaws. English were rivalling the French for this area.

MANSFIELD (DeSoto Parish)   *District 4, in town*

Keachi College
1856–1912

On this site stood a female college. Founded by Perry J. Backus of Good Hope (Keachi) Baptist Church on land donated by T. M. Gatlin. Became male and female institution in 1879. Served as hospital after Battle of Mansfield in 1864.

Sponsored by Keachi Heritage Foundation.

MANSFIELD (DeSoto Parish)   *District 4, in town*

Battle of Mansfield

Three miles east is site of the Battle of Mansfield, April 8, 1864, a decisive Confederate victory which led to the defeat of General Banks' Red River campaign and Federal evacuation at Grand Encore.

MANSURA (Avoyelles Parish)   *SH 114, District 8, in town*

Battle of Mansura

Confederate forces under General Dick Taylor here formed battle line May 16, 1864, barring passage of General Banks' retreating Union Army. The Battle of Mansura ended in withdrawal of Confederates.

MANSURA (Avoyelles Parish)   *District 8, in front of Desfosse House*

Desfosse House

Dr. Jules Charles Desfosse, 2nd mayor of Mansura, acquired this c. 1790 house and rebuilt it c. 1850. This Louisiana French Colonial style dwelling was the 1st structure in Avoyelles Parish listed on the National Register of Historic Places.

MANY (Sabine Parish)   *SH 6, District 8*

Fort Jesup

Established in 1822 by General Zachary Taylor as the major American fortification on the Southwestern frontier, and later became known as the Cradle of the Mexican War.

MANY (Sabine Parish)   *SH 6, District 8, near town*

Pendleton Crossing

Entrance to controversial Neutral Strip bounded by Sabine River West and Arroyo Hondo East. It was claimed by the United States after Louisiana Purchase, 1803, and by Spain as the ancient boundary of Mexico.

MARKSVILLE (Avoyelles Parish)   *District 8, Courthouse Square*

The First Bowie Knife

Rezin P. Bowie, brother of Alamo hero James Bowie, wrote, "The first Bowie knife was made by myself in the Parish of Avoyelles." With this knife James killed Norris Wright in the famous Sandbar Fight near Natchez Miss., Sept. 19, 1827.

MARKSVILLE (Avoyelles Parish)   *District 8, near town*

Fort De Russy

Fort De Russy, four miles north, potent Confederate stronghold defending lower Red River Valley, yielded to land attack of General A.J. Smith's Union Army on March 14, 1864.

MARKSVILLE (Avoyelles Parish)   *SH 1, District 8, in town*

Hypolite Bordelon House

This c. 1820 Creole house is typical of the dwellings of early Avoyelles Parish families. The Bordelon family, who built the house, was one of the parish's pioneer families. Listed on National Register of Historic Places in 1980.

MARKSVILLE (Avoyelles Parish)   *SH 1, District 8*

Indian Museum

One mile east on Old River is the restored Marksville Indian ceremonial center used about 500 A.D. Ancestors of Avoyle and Natches Tribes lived there until 1700 A.D.

MARKSVILLE (Avoyelles Parish) *SH 1, District 8*
The Marksville Site

One mile east is the Marksville prehistoric Indian ceremonial center. This site, occupied from 1–400 A.D., was related to the Ohio Hopewell Culture, and was noted for its elaborate trade networks and mortuary ceremonialism.

MARTHAVILLE (Natchitoches Parish) *District 8, near town*
Grave of Unknown Confederate Soldier

Here lies an unknown Confederate, killed by Union troops, April 2, 1864, during the Red River Campaign. This soldier had been cut off from his unit following a skirmish at nearby Crump's Hill. He was shot at this site while attempting to rejoin other Confederate troops.

MARTIN (Red River Parish) *District 4, in town*
Reverend John Dupree
1806–1899

Pioneer Baptist preacher and missionary. He organized many churches in Georgia as well as sixteen in Louisiana east of Red River, where his labors began in 1862. Traveled great distances on horseback. Baptized hundreds of converts.

MAUREPAS ISLAND (St. John the Baptist Parish)
Maurepas Island

Surrounded by Lake Maurepas, the Amite River, Bayou Pierre, the Petite Amite, and Blind River. Lake named by Iberville in 1699 for Comte de Maurepas. Area settled by French, Spanish, and German immigrants.

METAIRIE (Jefferson Parish) *District 2, junction of Metairie Rd. and 17th St. Canal*
Chartier Concession

Pierre Chartier de Baulne, French Louisiana attorney general in 1719, held the earliest land grant at the former village of the Colapissas on Chapitoulas (Metairie) Road. His family first colonists to live nearby.
Sponsored by Jefferson Parish Historical Commission.

METAIRIE (Jefferson Parish) *District 2, junction of Labarre and Metairie rds.*

Labarre Road

Named after de la Barre family. Francois Pascalis de La Barre I, a noted colonial official, owned a river to lake tract in 1750. Further family holdings, by 1800s, made Metairie called popularly "La Plaine Labarre."

Sponsored by Jefferson Parish Historical Commission.

MINDEN (Webster Parish) *US 79, District 4, in town*

Germantown Colony

About 7 miles northeast on Route 186 are remnants of colony founded 1835 by followers of Count Leon, who came from Germany to America for a religious belief. There, they operated a communal village until 1871.

MINDEN (Webster Parish) *US 79, District 4, near town*

Memorial Shrine

In memory of our pioneer settlers who built near here the first church, schoolhouse, seat of government, post office, and cemetery. Here the first white child born in this Minden area is buried.

MONROE (Ouachita Parish) *District 5, in town at 438 S. Grand*

Fort Miro

Original stockade built on this site in 1790 by Commandant Jean Filhiol and Lieut. Joseph de la Baume of Ouachita District. Half of timbers furnished by officers; half by garrison and settlers.

MONROE (Ouachita Parish) *District 5, in town*

Indian Village

On this site, granted by the Spanish government, dwelled Tusquahoma, chief of a Choctaw Indian tribe of fifty families, from about 1785 to 1820, when the land was sold to Stephen Maddox and the tribe moved west.

MONTPELIER (St. Helena Parish)   *District 62, in town*

Montpelier

Parish seat from 1812–1832. Land office—a clearinghouse for public lands between the Mississippi and the Pearl Rivers 1812–1837. Montpelier Academy 1833–1840. Early post office St. Helena 1814–1859. Connected to Natchez Trace.

MORGAN CITY (St. Mary Parish)   *District 3, in town*

Attakapa Militia

The Militia of the Attakapa Region of South Central Louisiana served under Spain's Governor of the colony, Bernardo de Galvez, in his campaigns against the British during the War for American Independence.

MORGAN CITY (St. Mary Parish)   *District 3, in town*

Dr. Walter Brashear
B. MD 1776—D. LA 1860

Famed as surgeon in Ky. 1806. Settled Attakapas, La. 1809. Became larger landowner, sugar planter in St. Mary, serving many years in La. Legislature. Town of Brashear, now Morgan City, incorporated 1860.

MORGAN CITY (St. Mary Parish)   *US 90, District 3, in town*

Fort Brashear
(also known as Fort Star)

Located one half mile south. This Union fort was the scene of an important military engagement on June 23, 1863, resulting in the Confederate capture of 700 Federal troops and immense military stores.

MORGAN CITY (St. Mary Parish)   *US 90, District 3, in town*

Morgan City

4th port of La. Shrimp, oil, gas center. Early gateway from the Mississippi to Teche. Site of Tiger Island plantation of Dr. Walter Brashear, 1860; renamed 1876, for Charles Morgan who made the port a leading steamboat, railroad hub.

NAPOLEONVILLE (Assumption Parish)   *District 61, in front of church*

Christ Episcopal Church

Site from Elm Hall Plantation donated by Dr. E. E. Kittredge. Congregation organized and church constructed in 1853. Frank Willis, Architect. Consecrated by the Rt. Rev. Leonidas K. Polk in 1854. W. W. Pugh, Warden, 1853–1905.

NAPOLEONVILLE (Assumption Parish)   *SH 308, District 61, near town*

Madewood Plantation House

The first major building designed by noted architect Henry Howard. Construction of this Greek Revival mansion was begun in 1846, using materials from the land. Steamboats carried trade to Madewood on Bayou Lafourche.

NAPOLEONVILLE (Assumption Parish)   *District 61, Bayou Lafourche Hwy.*

Napoleonville

Named for the Emperor of France. An early travel route, 1730–70, used by the French then Acadians from St. James to the Attakapas Landing on Lake Verret. Lake was named for Nicholas Verret family of St. James and Assumption Parishes where father and son served as Commandants.

NATCHITOCHES (Natchitoches Parish)   *River Rd., District 8, in front of house*

Badin-Roque House

Rare surviving example of a poteaux-en-terre (posts in the ground) house, an ancient form of construction prevalent in Mississippi Valley during 18th and 19th centuries. Probably fewer than 10 extant examples in U.S.

NATCHITOCHES (Natchitoches Parish)   *SH 1, District 8*

The City of Natchitoches

Founded by St. Denis, 1714; the oldest permanent settlement in Louisiana and the entire Louisiana Purchase territory west of the Mississippi. On this site, Fort St. Jean Baptiste was built about 1715.

NATCHITOCHES (Natchitoches Parish)   *District 8, hill on*
                                           Northwestern State College

Colonial Gateway Corral

First sighted by St. Denis and Bienville in 1700, this hill was later St. Denis' vacherie. Here three paths met. From the Spanish West came cattle and horses; eastward were his home and the route of flatboats to New Orleans. A road wound north to the Fort.

NATCHITOCHES (Natchitoches Parish)   *SH 1, District 8, in town*

Fort St. Jean Baptiste

Built about 1715 by request of Saint Denis to halt the Spanish expansion eastward. Natchitoches Indians, allies of the French, gave their name to the city.

NATCHITOCHES (Natchitoches Parish)   *District 8, west side of*
                                           SH 1 bypass, on rise adjacent to
                                           NSU Recreation Complex

Francois Rouquier Homesite

At this location stood the home of Francois Rouquier, early Natchitoches Indian trader and farmer. The house foundations, dating to circa 1780, were uncovered during archaeological excavations undertaken in 1975.

NATCHITOCHES (Natchitoches Parish)   *District 8, in town*

Henri de Tonti

On Feb. 17, 1690, Henri de Tonti, a trader and French army officer known as the Iron Hand, arrived in this area to search for La Salle's lost colony. While here, he helped arrange a treaty between the Taensa and Natchitoches Indians.

NATCHITOCHES (Natchitoches Parish)   *SH 6, District 8, in town*

Los Adais

On this hill Spain erected a fort that served as Capital of the Province of Texas from 1721 to 1773. The only Spanish Mission in this area was erected on the opposite hill in 1717, soon after the French founded Natchitoches.

NATCHITOCHES (Natchitoches Parish)
District 8, on Second St.

Site of Fort Claiborne

Fort established here in 1804. Named after Wm. C. C. Claiborne, then governor of territorial Louisiana. Protected U.S. interests on southwestern frontier. Garrisoned almost continuously until establishment of Fort Jesup in 1822.

NATCHITOCHES (Natchitoches Parish)
SH 6, District 8, north of town, near Grand Encore Bridge

Site of Fort Selden

About 2 miles NW. Occupied 1816–17 and 1819–22. Purpose was to police southwestern frontier and guard Red River and Bayou Pierre. Gen. Edmund P. Gaines, commander of the Western Department, had his head-quarters here for a time.

NEWELLTON (Tensas Parish)
District 58, Linwood Plantation

Linwood Plantation

Near this site was the Taensa village, visited by de LaSalle, Tonti, Father Membre in 1682 explorations. In 1699–1700 Father de Montigny made peace between the Taensa and Natchez and established a mission. By 1706 the Taensa were forced to move by the Chickasaw and Yazoo.

NEW IBERIA (Iberia Parish)
US 90, District 3, in town

Bayou Teche

Name comes from Indian legend that writhing snake (Tenche) made stream bed, or from "Deutch" after German settlers. Approx. 80 miles long, bayou starts near Port Barre, converges with Atchafalaya near Morgan City. Important waterway in Louisiana history for Indians, traders, settlers.

NEW IBERIA (Iberia Parish)
SH 86 from SH 31, District 3

Belmont Plantation

Land was an original Spanish Grant to Francois Pellerin. Property then owned successively by the Sterling, Peebles, and finally the Wyche families.

This plantation has produced sugar since late 19th century and is site of unusual water-powered sugar mill. The house was destroyed by fire in 1947.

NEW IBERIA (Iberia Parish)   *SH 541, District 3, on East Main St.*
Frederick Larned Gates

Former home of Frederick Larned Gates (1827–1897), outstanding citizen, businessman, lawyer, and Civil War veteran. He served as district judge in the 1870s and 1880s. As an early industrialist, Gates developed a cotton seed oil business which was one of the area's major enterprises.

NEW IBERIA (Iberia Parish)   *District 3, near town, corner of East St. Peter and Wecks sts.*
Hadrian, Roman Emperor
117 A.D.–138 A.D.

Noted as a builder and financier. This one-ton antiquity sculpted from life in 127 A.D. Came to Iberia in 1961 from Rome via London and New Orleans.

NEW IBERIA (Iberia Parish)   *District 3, at Mt. Carmel Academy*
Mt. Carmel Academy

An educational institution for girls established in 1872 by the Sisters of Mt. Carmel. The order was founded in 1825 in Tours, France. The old building which is nearest Bayou Teche was constructed by Henry F. Duperier in 1826.
Sponsored by Students of Mt. Carmel and Attkapas Historical Association.

NEW IBERIA (Iberia Parish)   *US 90, District 3, in town*
New Iberia

Early in 1779 Governor Bernardo de Galvez sent Lieutenant Colonel Francisco Bouligny with nearly five hundred Spanish and Canary Island Colonists to establish a settlement on the lower Bayou Teche in the Attakapas Country. These Spanish Colonists named their settlement New Iberia, for their own Iberian Peninsula.

NEW IBERIA (Iberia Parish)   *US 90 East, District 3, in town*
Old Spanish Trail

Named in honor of the Spanish Pioneers who for a period during the Colonial Era occupied the entire Southern region of the United States from St. Augustine to San Diego.

NEW IBERIA (Iberia Parish)   *District 3, in town*
Spanish Lake

First known as Lake Flamand for Jean B. Grevenberg, one of the earliest settlers in this area; called Lake Tasse by the French because of its round cup shape, and later known as Spanish Lake for the Seguras, Romeros, Villatoros, and others who lived on its shores.

NEW IBERIA (Iberia Parish)   *In town*
St. John the Evangelist Church Parish

Founded 12 January 1879 by Napoleon J. Perche, Archbishop of New Orleans. The present church was built in 1908, Rev. M. Bardy, pastor, August 1885–June 1928.

NEW ORLEANS (Orleans Parish)   *District 2,*
City Park and Carrollton Ave.

Allard Plantation

Plantation of Louis Allard was purchased by his grandfather, Don Santiago Lorreins in 1770s from estate of Francisco Hery, called Duplanty, builder of the first Cabildo Building in N.O. in 1769. Acquired from Allard in 1845 by J. McDonough—given to N.O. in 1850.

NEW ORLEANS (Orleans Parish)   *District 2, 200 Magazine St.*
Bienville's Plantation

Here, on a plantation granted to him on March 27, 1719, by the company of the Indies, stood the residence of Jean Baptiste Lemoyne de Bienville, founder of New Orleans. This plantation was sold by Bienville on April 11, 1726, to the Jesuit Fathers from whom it was confiscated in 1763.

NEW ORLEANS (Orleans Parish)   *District 2, in Audubon Park*

Bore Plantation—Audubon Park

This site 1781–1820 Plantation of Jean Etienne Bore (1741–1820), First Mayor of N.O. 1803–1804. Here Bore first granulated sugar in 1795. Purchased for park in 1871. Site of World's Industrial and Cotton Centennial Exposition 1884–1885.

NEW ORLEANS (Orleans Parish)   *Esplanade Ave., District 2,*
                                          corner of Tonti Street at Gayarre Place

Edgar Germain Hilaire Degas

French "impressionist" master whose mother and grandmother were born in New Orleans. Painted many famous subjects on a visit here in 1872–1873 at Musson Home on Esplanade. His "Portrait of Estelle" bought by Delgado Museum.

NEW ORLEANS (Orleans Parish)   *District 2, between*
                                          Robert E. Lee and Lakeshore

Fort St. John (Spanish Fort)

Established by Colonial French in the early 18th century. Rebuilt by the Spanish—1779. American restoration—1808. Built to protect New Orleans from attack by way of Lake Ponchartrain.

NEW ORLEANS (Orleans Parish)   *District 2, in town on Esplanade St.*

Fort St. Charles

On Oct. 25, 1769, under Gen. O'Reilly, Spanish Governor of Louisiana, were executed French patriots and martyrs: de Lafreniere, Marquis, Noyan, Caresse, Milhet, Villere having died previously.

NEW ORLEANS (Orleans Parish)   *District 2, downtown,*
                                          lakeside corner of
                                          Prytania and Washington aves.

Garden District

Famous for its 19th century homes and gardens, this area was originally part of Livaudais Plantation. Became part of City of Lafayette, 1833.

Annexed by City of New Orleans, 1852. Designated National Historic Landmark, 1974.

NEW ORLEANS (Orleans Parish)   *District 2, at 1122 Jackson*
Goldsmith-Godchaux House

Designed by noted nineteenth century architect Henry Howard in 1859. Significant for its painted interiors. Has more fresco wall decoration and stenciling than probably any other mid-nineteenth century residence in the South.

NEW ORLEANS (Orleans Parish)   *District 2, in town*
Jefferson City

Originally a part of Jefferson Parish, this area was incorporated as Jefferson City in 1850. By 1860 its population was 5,107, including 131 free black citizens. It was annexed by the City of New Orleans in 1870.

NEW ORLEANS (Orleans Parish)   *In town*
Lafayette Square

Planned in 1788 as a public place for Faubourg Ste. Marie, the City's first suburb, this Square honors American Revolutionary War Hero, Marie Joseph Paul Ives Roch Gilbert Du Motier, Marquis de Lafayette. He declined the invitation to become the first Governor when the United States purchased Louisiana. During his April 9–15, 1825, visit to the City of New Orleans, his popularity was evidenced by resounding cheers of "Vive Lafayette, Vive Lafayette." [Bilingual.]
Sponsored by France-Amerique de la Louisiane, Inc.

NEW ORLEANS (Orleans Parish)   *District 2, St. Bernard and*
Lakeshore Ave.

Lake Pontchartrain

Traveled on by Iberville, 1699, and named for the French Minister of Marine. Indians called it Okwa-ta, wide water. First port of embarkation was at the site where Bayou St. John flows from this lake. It was the first water travel route to the City of New Orleans.

NEW ORLEANS (Orleans Parish) *At the Moon Walk in town*

La Salle Claims Louisiana

On April 9, 1682, Rene-Robert Cavelier de La Salle claimed the Mississippi Valley (from the Gulf of Mexico to Canada) in the name of the French king, christening the territory "Louisiana" for Louis XIV.

NEW ORLEANS (Orleans Parish) *District 2, Moss St. and City Park Ave.*

Metairie and Gentilly Ridges

First highway through this city led from lower Kenner to Chef Menteur. Mississippi River, during prehistoric days, overflowed into Lake Pontchartrain. The receding of waters created these ridges and their accompanying bayous which connected, at City Park area, with Bayou St. John.

NEW ORLEANS (Orleans Parish) *District 2, in City Park*

New Orleans

First sighted as Indian portage to Lake Ponchartrain and Gulf in 1699 by Bienville and Iberville. Founded by Bienville in 1718; named by him in honor of the Duke of Orleans, Regent of France. Called the Crescent City because of location in bend of the Mississippi.

NEW ORLEANS (Orleans Parish) *District 2, in town*

The Old Mortuary Chapel

Built in 1826 as a burial church for victims of yellow fever, the chapel is oldest surviving church in the city. Now Our Lady of Guadalupe, the chapel is the official chapel of the New Orleans Police and Fire Departments.

NEW ORLEANS (Orleans Parish) *District 2, Moss and Graude*

The Old Portage

Short trail from Lake Ponchartrain to River shown by Indians to Iberville and Bienville, 1699. Winding trail used by early travelers to city. From Bayou St. John it led to N. Broad, Bayou Roads, Vieux Carre to Mississippi River at site between Dumaine and Gov. Nicholls sts.

NEW ORLEANS (Orleans Parish)   *District 2, on Moss St.*

Pitot House

Built late 18th century. Home of James Pitot who was first mayor of incorporated city of New Orleans, 1804–1805. Also builder of one of the city's first cotton presses.

NEW ORLEANS (Orleans Parish)   *District 2, on the neutral ground of St. Charles Ave. in 8000 block*

The St. Charles Line

Began service in 1835 as the Carrollton Line of the N.O. & Carrollton Railroad. Powered by steam engine, horse, and mule prior to electrification in 1893. It is the oldest continuously operated street railway line in the world.

NEW ORLEANS (Orleans Parish)   *District 2, on Decatur St.*

The Steamer *New Orleans*

On January 10, 1812, the steamer *New Orleans,* commanded by Nicholas Roosevelt, arrived on this spot. It was the first steamboat to successfully navigate the Ohio and Mississippi Rivers. Steamboats were a major factor in the growth of New Orleans as a world port.

NEW ORLEANS (Orleans Parish)   *District 2, in town*

Storyville

Created 1897 and closed 1917, New Orleans' famous legalized red-light district was in this area. Among many great jazz musicians on the scene here were "King" Oliver, "Jelly Roll" Morton, Louis Armstrong, Tony Jackson, and Jimmie Noone.

NEW ORLEANS (Orleans Parish)   *US 90, District 2, in town*

"To A Point Called Chef Menteur"

1763 grant to Col. Gilbert A. de St. Maxent along Bayou Gentilly. Became known as Maxent-DeClouet-LaFon-Michoud Tract; in 1923, "Faubourg de Montluzin"; bought by "New Orleans East, Inc.," 1959. NASA Missile Plant, Michoud Operations located there, 9/7/1961.

NEW ORLEANS (Orleans Parish)   *District 2, neutral ground of*
Carrollton Ave. between Hampson
and Burthe sts.

Town of Carrollton

Laid out by Charles Zimpel in 1833 on site of Macarty Plantation, formerly uppermost part of Bienville's 1719 land grant. Jefferson Parish seat 1852–1874. Annexed 1874 by New Orleans. 1854 courthouse designed by Henry Howard.

NEW ORLEANS (Orleans Parish)   *3029 St. Charles Ave.,*
in front of Van-Benthuysen Mansion

Van Benthuysen-Elms Mansion

(Attributed to Lewis E. Reynolds, Architect.) Built 1869 for "Yankee in Grey," Capt. Watson Van Benthuysen, II, CSA. Relative by marriage of Jefferson Davis and Q'master of Presidential convoy that fled Richmond in April 1865, Van B. became merchant and industrialist with interests in St. Charles streetcar line, telephone company, and firm that bridged Hudson at Poughkeepsie. Born NY 1833, Van B. died here 1901. Gr'daughter Mae Van B. became Queen of Carnival 1902. House served as German Consulate General 1931–41. From here, Baron Edgar von Spiegel, novelist and U-boat kapitan, informed Axis submarines of ship departures. Became John Elms family residence 1951.

NEW ORLEANS (Orleans Parish)   *District 2, in town on Canal St.*

Vieux Carre Forts

Site of Fort St. Louis, upstream bastion of New Orleans, founded 1717 by Bienville and laid out by Adrien de Pauger. Other forts: St. Charles, St. Jean, St. Ferdinand, and Burgogne.

NEW SARPY (Jefferson Parish)   *SH 48, District 2, in town*

L'ansse Aux Outardes

Bustard's Cove, 1722. Settled by Canadians, French. Bienville came here in 1699 from Lake Ponchartrain using small waterways, portage. LeSueur and Canadians used the route and were met here by Iberville and Tonti Feb. 24, 1700. It became part of the "Second German Coast" about 1730.

OAK GROVE (West Carroll Parish)   *SH 17/2, District 5, in town*

Lane's Ferry

Near this point in 1700 Jean Baptiste le Moyne de Bienville, colonizer and first governor of Louisiana, crossed Bayou Macon en route to the trading post on the Ouachita.

OIL CITY (Caddo Parish)   *SH 1, District 4, in Earl Williamson Park*

Huddie "Leadbelly" Ledbetter

Blues singer from Mooringsport, La. (1888–1949). He played 12-string guitar on Shreveport's Fannin St., sang his way out of prison, and became a folk hero with songs like "Goodnight Irene," "Bourgeois Blues," and "Midnight Special."

OPELOUSAS (St. Landry Parish)

Black Academy at Mt. Olive Baptist Church
(1897–1918)

In 1897, when there were few local schools for Blacks, the 7th District Baptist School was founded and housed in the original church building on this site. It was one of two private schools for area Blacks.

OPELOUSAS (St. Landry Parish)   *US 190, District 3, in town*

Opelousas

Poste des Opelousas founded by French traders middle of 18th century. Headquarters district of Opelousas under Spanish 1769. Parish seat of "Old Imperial St. Landry" 1808. State Capital 1862–63.

OPELOUSAS (St. Landry Parish)   *SH 182, District 3, in town*

Site of Bowie Residence

James Bowie lived here with his family from 1815 to 1824. The Bowies operated several sawmills along the bayous of St. Landry Parish. The famous Bowie knife became a legend in Opelousas prior to his heroic death at the Alamo.

PATOUTVILLE (St. Mary Parish) *District 3, near Jeanerette off US 90, Old St. Nicholas Church Square*

Enterprise Plantation

Established by Pierre Simeon Patout in 1825. Originally intended as a vineyard, the plantation was converted to sugar cane. It is the oldest complete working sugar cane plantation in the United States.

PATTERSON (St. Mary Parish) *SH 182, District 3, Patterson Airport*

Williams Memorial Airport

Here from 1929 until 1936, Harry P. Williams and James R. Wedell, as Wedell-Williams Air Service, designed and built some of the fastest land-based airplanes of their time. "Jimmie" Wedell set many flying records, winning the Bendix & Thompson Trophies.

PHOENIX (Plaquemines Parish) *SH 39, District 2, in town*

Fort De La Boulaye

First white settlement in present-day Louisiana, erected by Bienville in 1699 on this spot (then the bank of the Mississippi), prevented Britain's seizure of the Mississippi Valley.

PINEVILLE (Rapides Parish) *US 165, District 8, in town*

Bailey's Dam

About ½ mile downstream is the site of Col. Joseph Bailey's noted dam, which allowed escape on May 13, 1864, of the Federal Fleet of some 35 vessels under the command of Admiral David A. Porter.

PINEVILLE (Rapides Parish) *District 8, in town*

City of Pineville

In 1722 Diron d'Artaguette, Inspector of Troops in Louisiana, recommended the establishment of a fortified post on Red River to prevent Indian attacks on those portaging the rapids. Although it is probable that some type of French presence was established near the rapids shortly after the Inspector's report, the specific date of origin for "Post du Rapide" was not until 1770. Eight years following Louisiana's transfer to Spain in 1762, Etienne

Layssard was appointed the post commandant. A census commissioned by Gen. Alexandro O-Reilly in 1769 reported about 100 settlers, including slaves and Apache Indians near the post. By the late 18th century numerous families from Virginia, Maryland, Georgia, and the Carolinas had settled in the vicinity, taking advantage of liberal land grants extended by the Spanish government. Prior to U.S. annexation by the Louisiana "Purchase" in 1803, the post served as portage station along Nolan's Trace, a trail blazed in the horse trade between Spanish Texas and the American Southwest. In the early 19th century an influx of merchants, farmers, and herdsmen gave rise to the community of "Pineville." Throughout the century Pineville served as an important commercial link to towns and villages north of the Red River. On March 14, 1878, the town was incorporated.

Sponsored by Central Cities Development Corporation.

PINEVILLE (Rapides Parish)   *District 8, in town*
First United Methodist Church
Pineville, Louisiana

1802–1806	First Circuit Riders (ministers) began work in Louisiana.
1811	Rapides Circuit founded—Miles Harper presiding elder.
1814	John Schrock began work in Rapides area of Louisiana.
1817	Ashley Hewitt, Richmond Nolley, Jonathan C. Jones, and Alexander Whitney each active in Methodism in Rapides area.
1849	Louisiana Conference founded, minutes listed Pineville as preaching stop for circuit preachers.
1873	3 acres donated by Thomas E. Maddox to J. M. Henry for the purpose of building a church and cemetery in Pineville.
1875	The Methodist Church and cemetery is located at the corner of Singer and Hardtner streets.
1916	Church moved to 800 block of Main Street, known as Little White Church House. The pews and stained-glass windows were from the original church.
1927	Church moved to 900 block of Main Street and built a two-story brick building.
1939	The Methodist Episcopal Church, North, and Protestant, formed Methodist Church. Present congregation became part of South Central jurisdiction.

1951	Groundbreaking for educational building at 101 College Boulevard.
1960	First worship service in new sanctuary on Easter Sunday, April 17th.
1973	Wilson Watson Building opened as part of church plant.
1974	George W. Dameron Memorial Library established in church.
1984	Damaged church steeple replaced and church plant expanded.

Sponsored by the First United Methodist Church of Pineville.

PINEVILLE (Rapides Parish) — *District 8, on Main St.*
The Jewish Cemetery

The earliest known Jewish settler in the Alexandria-Pineville area was Henry Michael Hyams, whose name appears in the 1830 census.

The earliest grave marker identifiable on this site tells that Augusta Bernstein, daughter of Samuel Bernstein, was buried here after her death on September 19, 1852. At least six other early burials were of victims of the 1853 yellow fever epidemic.

The Hebrew Benevolent Association of Rapides, also known as Congregation Gemiluth Chassodim, was chartered October 2, 1859. The first officers were Isaac Levy, President; Henry Greenwood, Vice-President; Julius Levin, Secretary; M. Steinfels, Treasurer; and B. Weiss, M. L. Wagner, and A. Sterne, Directors.

According to a re-recorded deed, land for this cemetery was sold to this association on January 15, 1861, by Bertha Mitchell Weinberg, Henry Klotz, and Samuel Bernstein.

Sponsored by Jewish Welfare Federation of Central Louisiana.

PINEVILLE (Rapides Parish) — *SH 28 East, District 8*
Kees Park

Edward J. Barrett, an Irishman who was a soldier in the Federal Army of Occupation which was billeted in Pineville for two years after the conclusion of the Civil War, chose to remain and in 1868 married a local girl, Mary Reagan. He was later elected to the Louisiana State Legislature and served on the Rapides Parish School Board, Police Jury, Pineville Town Council, and as Mayor of the Town of Pineville. On May 15, 1920, Barrett gave the land which includes this Park to Right Reverend Cornelius Van de Ven, Bishop of Alexandria, for use by the Roman Catholic Church. A small monastery and church were built, and the area was named Grace Park. Bishop Van de Ven and several priests were buried in Grace Park. The Most Reverend Charles P. Greco sold the land to Central Louisiana Electric Company on August 10, 1951, and the mission and cemetery were subsequently moved. The City was permitted to use the land from 1952 until it was donated by CLECO to the City on June 2, 1959. The Park was renamed May 6, 1952, in honor of William "Billy" Ezra Kees, Sr. who was born June 11, 1881, as the son of Jesse M. and Nannie Cooper Kees. Billy Kees married Julia Elizabeth "Doll" Bradford in 1905, and he was appointed postmaster in 1911, when the post office was located in the Kees General Store on Red River. He was active in various civic, educational, and church affairs in Pineville and died April 14, 1938.

Sponsored by the Stafford G. Kees family.

PINEVILLE (Rapides Parish)   *District 8, in town*

Louisiana College

The roots of Louisiana College extend to schools at Mount Lebanon (Bienville Parish) and Keachie (DeSoto Parish), founded in the 1850s by north Louisiana Baptists. By the end of the nineteenth century the Louisiana Baptist Convention (LBC) assumed control over both institutions and at the same time began to plan for a more centrally located college. In January 1906, the Education Commission of the LBC voted in favor of this site over land offered in Alexandria, and on October 3rd of the same year Louisiana College opened with 19 students and 3 faculty members. In 1909 the school became coeducational. After a devastating fire on January 3, 1911, sentiment arose among some Baptist leaders for relocation of the college, but later in the year at a special session of the LBC, delegates voted overwhelmingly to rebuild at the Pineville site. In 1923 Louisiana College became one of the first colleges in the state to receive accreditatiton from the Southern Association of Colleges & Secondary Schools.

Sponsored by Central Cities Development Corporation.

PINEVILLE (Rapides Parish)   *District 8, in town*
Mt. Olivet Episcopal Church

Completed and consecrated in 1859 by Bishop Leonidas Polk. Construction supervised by Charles Schraeder, a native of Germany. Wife of Rev. Amos D. McCoy of church in Alexandria initiated the construction of the chapel.

PLAQUEMINE (Iberville Parish)   *In town*
Old City Hall

Iberville Parish Courthouse, 1848–1906; Plaquemine City Hall, 1906–85. Built by George and Thomas Weldon of Mississippi. One of Louisiana's oldest public buildings. Listed on National Register of Historic Places.
Sponsored by Iberville Parks and Recreation District.

PONCHATOULA (Tangipahoa Parish)   *District 62, in front of depot*
Ponchatoula Depot

Original depot built c. 1854 by New Orleans, Jackson & Great Northern Railroad (later Illinois Central). Burned when Union forces captured town in March 1863. Rebuilt c. 1865. Present depot built in 1894 and remodeled in the 1920s.

PORT ALLEN (West Baton Rouge Parish)   *US 90, District 61, in town*
Allendale Plantation

Home of Second Louisiana Confederate Governor Henry Watkins Allen. Purchased from Colonel William Nolan in 1852 for $300,000, which included 125 slaves. House burned by Federal troops during the War.

PORT ALLEN (West Baton Rouge Parish)   *District 61,*
                                                  corner of SH 986 and SH 415
Rosedale Road (LA Hwy. 986)

Over the Rosedale Road in May 1864 marched the Union army of Major General Nathaniel P. Banks on its return to New Orleans following the failure of the Red River Campaign.

PORT BARRE (St. Landry Parish) *US 90, District 3, in town*

Port Barre

Busy port during steamboat days; named after the Barre family. In 1765 Charles Barre bought 8,800 arpents from Jacque Guillaume Courtableau, 1st Commandant, Opelousas Post. Here Bayou Courtableau gives birth to Bayou Teche.

PORT HUDSON (East Baton Rouge Parish) *SH 48, District 61, in town*

Port Hudson

Seven miles west is site of anchor fort controlling Mississippi. Here 6,500 Confederates held 30,000 Union troops May 21 until July 8, 1863. Fall of Port Hudson opened river, hastening fall of Confederacy.

PORT SULPHUR (Plaquemines Parish) *SH 23, District 2, in front of Freeport's Port Sulphur facilities*

Port Sulphur

Hub of the Louisiana sulphur industry. Built in 1932–33 by Freeport Sulphur Company to logistically support Grande Ecaille mine, world's second largest Frasch sulphur mine. It was located in Lake Washington, 10 miles SW. *Sponsored by Plaquemines Parish Historical Society.*

PORT VINCENT (Livingston Parish) *District 62, in town*

Port Vincent

Originally a Spanish settlement and early port on Amite River route from Mississippi River via Bayou Manchac. First called Scivicque's Ferry for Vincent Scivicque, native of Italy. Site of parish courthouse 1872–1881.

PRAIRIEVILLE (Ascension Parish) *US 61, District 61, in town*

Bayou Manchac (Iberville River)

Iberville returned from Mississippi River to his fleet at Ship Island via this bayou in 1699. Boundary: Spanish Isle of Orleans and British West Florida, 1763–1783, and Territory of Orleans and Spanish District of Baton Rouge, 1803–1810.

RAYNE (Acadia Parish)   *In town*
Pouppeville
Named for the merchant Jules Poupppeville and dating back to the 1850s, Pouppeville was once a stagecoach stop. The town was disassembled, carried north by oxen one mile to meet the railroad, and rebuilt at Rayne Station in 1881.

ROOSEVELT (East Carroll Parish)   *District 5, in town*
Roosevelt
Originally named O'Hara's Switch. Renamed Roosevelt in honor of President Theodore Roosevelt, who hunted bear in the area in October 1907. He recorded his adventures here in an article entitled "In the Louisiana Canebrakes."

ROSEDALE (Iberville Parish)   *District 61, in town*
Calumet Plantation
Home of Douglass C. Montan (1834–96), who named this plantation "Calumet" after Indian name for peace-pipe. Montan represented Iberville and West Baton Rouge Parishes in the La. State Senate. Montan wrote (1856) a popular book entitled "Redstick" which was about Baton Rouge life.

SCOTLANDVILLE (East Baton Rouge Parish)   *District 61,*
                                                       Scenic Highway

Southern University
West 300 yards is first state Negro institution of higher learning. Founded New Orleans 1880; became land grant college 1890; moved to Baton Rouge 1914 with Dr. J. S. Clark, founder, as first president.

SHREVEPORT (Caddo Parish)   *District 4, in town*
Bennett & Cane Trading Post
Site of trading post established prior to July 1, 1832, by William Smith Bennett and his brother-in-law James Huntington Cane, both from New Hampshire, on the bluff where Shreveport was founded 1836.
Sponsored by Shreveport Sesquicentennial Commission.

SHREVEPORT (Caddo Parish)   *District 4, in town*
Caddo Agency House

On bluff, south of this road, is site of Caddo Agency House where Caddo Indians ceded about 1,000,000 acres to the U.S. for $80,000 on July 1, 1835. By this treaty, Indians also gave to Larkin Edwards, interpreter and friend, a tract of land that later became the site of Shreveport.

SHREVEPORT (Caddo Parish)   *SH 80, District 4, in town*
Cane-Bennett Bluff

Trading Post established before July 1, 1832, by James Cane and William Bennett. Residence of Gen. Kirby Smith, Comdr. Trans-Miss. Dept., CSA, last Confederate Army to surrender in 1865.

SHREVEPORT (Caddo Parish)   *District 4, Atkins entrance*
Centenary College of Louisiana

Founded 1825 at Jackson, La., by the State of Louisiana, the college was transferred to the Methodist Church in 1845. Relocated at Shreveport in 1908, Centenary is the oldest privately operated liberal arts college west of the Mississippi.

SHREVEPORT (Caddo Parish)   *District 4, in town*
Church of the Holy Cross Episcopal

Bishop Leonidas Polk conducted first Episcopal service in Shreveport March 24, 1829. St. Paul's Church formed 1845. Renamed Grace Church 1851. Renamed St. Mark's 1859. St. Mark's relocated 1954. Holy Cross organized 1954.

SHREVEPORT (Caddo Parish)   *District 4, in town*
Coates Bluff

Two blocks east is site of home of first settler, Larkin Edwards, 1803, James Coats, 1817, and John McLeod, 1835. It became the first local post office on April 10, 1838.

SHREVEPORT (Caddo Parish) *District 4, in town*

Confederate Ironclad *Missouri*

Built 1863 one block east at Cross Bayou, with railroad T-rail armor and guns from USS Indianola; surrendered at Alexandria June 3, 1865. CSN Webb aided in Indianola capture and was refitted here as a cotton-clad for dash to Gulf 1865.

Sponsored by Shreveport Sesquicentennial Commission.

SHREVEPORT (Caddo Parish) *District 4, North Market St. and Cross Bayou*

Confederate Navy Yard

One block west near mouth Cross Bayou at Red River the ironclad *Missouri* and ram Webb built. *Missouri* armored with railroad iron. In 1863 Webb fought U.S.S. *Indianola* near Vicksburg. *Missouri* was surrendered here May 1865.

SHREVEPORT (Caddo Parish) *District 4, in town*

Dodd College

Private liberal arts junior college for girls, 1927–1942. Founded by Dr. M. E. Dodd, Pastor, First Baptist Church, Shreveport. Two original buildings now part of First Baptist Church. President's Home located at 601 Ockley Drive.

Sponsored by Dodd College Alumnae Association.

SHREVEPORT (Caddo Parish) *In town, at lower end of Fannin St.*

1st Caddo Parish Courthouse

Louisiana legislature, in creating Caddo Parish in 1838, designated the house of Thomas Wallace located approximately 2.5 mi. northwesterly on the south shore of Wallace Lake, the first seat of justice or courthouse.

Sponsored by Caddo Parish Commission.

SHREVEPORT (Caddo Parish)   *District 4, in town*

Fort Humbug

Formerly Fort Turnbull, built by the Confederates to defend Shreveport, then Capital of Louisiana. In 1864, charred logs simulating cannon were used to deter Union forces from attacking.

SHREVEPORT (Caddo Parish)   *912 Commerce St.,*
80 feet south of this corner

Gen. E. Kirby Smith Residence

912 Commerce Street, 80 feet south of this corner, site of Benjamin L. Hodge home, where Gen. Smith lived 1863–65 while Commander of Trans-Miss. Dept. CSA. Built 1848; demolished 1960. Originally home of La. Supreme Court Judge Thomas T. Land.
Sponsored by Shreveport Sesquicentennial Commission.

SHREVEPORT (Caddo Parish)   *District 4, River Park*

The Great Raft

Captain Henry Miller Shreve came to Red River in 1833 to remove the log jam 165 miles long, extending from Loggy Bayou to Hurricane Bluffs; the removal of the raft by 1837 opened Red River to navigation and made Shreveport an important center of trade and gateway to the West.

SHREVEPORT (Caddo Parish)   *District 4, in front of church*

Holy Trinity Catholic Church

Established in 1856, Holy Trinity was moved to this site in 1858. Five of its priests lost their lives treating the victims of the Yellow Fever Epidemic of 1873. The present church, in Romanesque Revival style, was built in 1896.

SHREVEPORT (Caddo Parish)   *US 71, District 4, close to*
Bossier-Red River Parish line

Loggy Bayou—Red River

Nearest point of Federal advance on Shreveport during Civil War. About four miles to southwest near confluence of streams Confederates sank steamer New Falls City which blocked passage of Federal gunboats, April 10, 1864.

SHREVEPORT (Caddo Parish)   *NE corner of Milam and McNeil sts.*
2nd Caddo Parish Courthouse

Caddo Parish in 1839 rented space in Chas. A. Sewall's store located on this site for clerk and sheriff's offices, and rented similar space Apr.–Sept. 1840 in the Planter's Hotel behind this site facing Milam Street.
Sponsored by Caddo Parish Commission.

SHREVEPORT (Caddo Parish)   *District 4, in town*
Shreveport

Founded by Shreve Town Co., Feb. 4, 1837, named for Captain Henry Miller Shreve, who opened Red River to navigation, making the city a Southwest gateway and trading center.

SHREVEPORT (Caddo Parish)   *District 4, in town*
Strand Theatre

Built by Saenger brothers and Ehrlich brothers, Shreveport citizens, and theatre industry magnates. Designed by Emil Weil. Opened 1925. One of the few remaining grandiose movie-vaudeville theatres built in America in the 1920s.

SHREVEPORT (Caddo Parish)   *SW corner of Texas and Marshall sts.*
3rd Caddo Parish Courthouse

Parish Judge Washington Jenkins, on Nov. 4, 1840, sold his 2-story frame house to Caddo Parish for a courthouse. A jail replaced the kitchen. Courthouse was sold at foreclosure in 1855 at its own door.
Sponsored by Caddo Parish Commission.

SIMMESPORT (Avoyelles Parish)   *District 8, Civil War fort*
Battle of Yellow Bayou

Also known as Norwood's Plantation, fought May 18, 1864. Last battle of Banks' Red River Campaign. General Richard Taylor's Confederate army failed to prevent Union army crossing Atchafalaya River at Simmesport.

SLIDELL (St. Tammany Parish)   *In town*

City of Slidell Centennial
Nov. 13, 1888–Nov. 13, 1988

Named for diplomat and U.S. Senator John Slidell of Louisiana by son-in-law Baron Frederic Erlanger, one of the financiers of New Orleans and Northeastern Railroad. Incorporated Nov. 13, 1888.
Sponsored by Citizens of Slidell.

SLIDELL (St. Tammany Parish)   *In town, at the church*

First United Methodist Church

Oldest Methodist Assembly in Slidell. Founded in a brush arbor on Sept. 26, 1887, as Methodist Episcopal Church South. Joined the Louisiana Conference in 1894. Present site dedicated July 16, 1961.
Sponsored by Wesley Fellowship Class and Friends, First United Methodist Church.

SLIDELL (St. Tammany Parish)   *US 11, District 2, near town*

Fort Pike

Historic state monument ten miles west on US 90, was completed in 1828 to defend Rigolets Pass, approach through Lake Pontchartrain to New Orleans. Named after Brigadier General Zebulon Montgomery Pike.

SLIDELL (St. Tammany Parish)   *District 62, Indian Village Rd.,*
between US 190 and West Pearl River

Indian Village

In 1699 Bienville visited the Colapissa Indians who lived in this area. The Indians called the Pearl River "Taleatcha" ("rock river") because of pearls found in shells from its waters. The French found the river water good to drink.

SLIDELL (St. Tammany Parish)
In town

Slidell Town Hall and Jail

Built in 1907, this building replaced the original wooden jail and mayor's office. It was the town hall until 1954 and the jail until 1963. The town's fire engine was located in the addition from 1928 until 1954.
Sponsored by St. Tammany Historical Society.

SORREL (St. Mary Parish)
US 90, District 3,
between Jeanerette and Franklin

Sorrel

Site of one of the early ranches along the Old Cattle Route from Mexico to Vacherie on the Miss. Joseph Sorrel, in cattle business from 1750s, had land claims of over three thousand acres.

SOUTHDOWN (Terrebonne Parish)
SH 311, District 3,
in front of Southdown

Southdown Plantation House

First floor built c. 1859 by William J. Minor of Natchez, Mississippi. Second floor added in 1893 by Henry C. Minor. In 1920s Southdown management pioneered development of disease-resistant POJ sugarcane varieties.

SPANISH LAKE (Iberia Parish)
SH 182, District 3,

Site of Camp Pratt

From 1862–1863 Camp Pratt was official Confederate camp of conscription and instruction for South Louisiana. At one time as many as 3,000 conscripts here. A small compound for Union prisoners of war also located at the camp.

SPRINGFIELD (Livingston Parish)
District 62, east of SH 42,
north of town, in front of
Galilee Baptist Church

Haynes Settlement

One of oldest Black settlements in Livingston Parish; only one known to be shown on a map. Named for Haynes family. Property crossed by

Brakenridge and Thomas RRs. Galilee Baptist Church est. in 1884 by Rev. C. C. Clayton.

SPRINGFIELD (Livingston Parish) *District 62, at courthouse*

Springfield

Oldest town in Livingston Parish. Incorporated in 1838. Named for abundant ground water springs. Connected to old Natchez Trace. Site of a Spanish fort about 1800. Parish seat from 1835–1872. Old courthouse still stands.

ST. BERNARD (St. Bernard Parish) *District 2, Ducros Museum-Library*

Terre-Aux-Bouef

Here, in "Land of Oxen," in 1788 Governor Bernardo de Galvez appointed Commandant Pierre Phillippe de Marigny to parcel land on the bayou for Canary Islanders. Later Creole planters bought large estates on the bayou.

ST. FRANCISVILLE (West Feliciana Parish) *US 61/35, District 61, in town*

Audubon Memorial

Oakley Plantation, 3 miles east, where John James Audubon painted 32 of his "Birds of America." It was built in 1799 by Ruffin Gray and acquired as a state park in 1947 from Miss Lucy Mathews.

ST. FRANCISVILLE (West Feliciana Parish) *District 61, Bayou Sara*

Bayou Sara

Called New Valencia by the Spanish, was one of earliest towns in Florida Parishes. Bayou Sara was the river port for the Felicianas and was one of the largest shipping points between Natchez and New Orleans before 1860.

ST. FRANCISVILLE (West Feliciana Parish) *US 61, District 61, near Bains*

The Cottage

Home of Thomas Butler (1785–1847), distinguished judge and planter in West Feliciana Parish; member of United States Congress (1818–1821);

served as president of the first Board of Trustees, for College of Louisiana, located at Jackson, which later became Centenary College.

ST. FRANCISVILLE (West Feliciana Parish)

District 61, church grounds

Grace Episcopal Church

As one of Louisiana's oldest Protestant Churches, its history began 1827 in St. Francisville; Investure came in 1829, with Bishop Polk's Visitation in 1839. Shelled during Civil War, the Church began to rebuild with final restoration in 1880s.

ST. FRANCISVILLE (West Feliciana Parish)

US 61, District 61, near town

Locust Grove

Cemetery four miles east is the burial place of Sarah Knox Davis, daughter of President Zachary Taylor and first wife of Jefferson Davis, President, Confederate States of America.

ST. FRANCISVILLE (West Felicians Parish)   *US 61, District 61, in town*

Lt. Commander John E. Hart

In nearby Grace Church Cemetery is the tomb of Lieut. Commander John E. Hart, U.S. Gunboat Albatross, buried at Episcopal service and with naval and masonic honors by Brother Masons of Feliciana Lodge No. 31 F.&A.M., June 11, 1863.

ST. FRANCISVILLE (West Feliciana Parish)

District 61, Rosedown Plantation

Rosedown Plantation

Spanish land grant made in 1789 to John Mills, American Revolutionary soldier. (Founder of Bayou Sara in 1790, Mills was also a leader in the West Florida Rebellion, 1810.) Daniel Turnbull built the present home at Rosedown in 1835.

ST. FRANCISVILLE (West Feliciana Parish) *District 61, in town*
St. Francisville

Site of early Houmas and Tunica Indian villages. French St. Reyne Concession, 1717; later abandoned. British and Spanish Colonial Eras, 1763–1810; Independent State of West Florida; annexed by U.S. in 1810.

ST. FRANCISVILLE (West Feliciana Parish) *District 61, in town*
West Feliciana Railroad

One of South's earliest railroads. Ran from St. Francisville, La., to Woodville, Ms. Idea conceived in 1828 as means of transporting cotton to river. Chartered in 1831. Completed in 1842. In use in Illinois Central System until abandoned in 1978.

ST. GABRIEL (Iberville Parish) *In town*
St. Gabriel
1761–1763

Church of the Iberville Coast built by Acadian exiles in 1769. It was located in 1773 on Spanish Manchac on a grant given by that government. German settlers came from Maryland in 1784.

ST. JAMES (St. James Parish) *SH 18, District 2*
Site of First Acadian Settlers in Louisiana

Refugees came overland 1756–57. In vicinity was 1762 grant to Jacques Cantrelle, Sr., of France after whom Church and Parish were named. Section once included in Les Oumas, Eveche of Quebec.

ST. JOSEPH (Tensas Parish) *District 58, in town*
St. Joseph

Tensas Parish seat since parish created in 1843. Rare example, for Deep South, of town planned and constructed around New England style village green. Historic district listed on National Register of Historic Places.

ST. MARTINVILLE (St. Martin Parish)   *District 3, at Evangeline Oak*
Evangeline Oak

Longfellow's poem "Evangeline" immortalized the tragedy of the Acadian exile from Nova Scotia in 1755. This oak marks the legendary meeting place of Emmeline Labiche and Louis Arceneaux, the counterparts of Evangeline and Gabriel.

ST. MARTINVILLE (St. Martin Parish)   *District 3, in town*
Oak and Pine Alley

Charles Durand, pre-Civil War sugar planter, credited with planting this alley. In legend a family wedding party rode down the alley canopied by giant spider webs dusted gold and silver. c. 1795–99 Spanish grant to Jacques Fontenette.

ST. MARTINVILLE (St. Martin Parish)   *District 3, in front of St. Martin de Tours Catholic Church*

St. Martinville

City developed c. 1795–c. 1900 through unusual semi-feudal arrangement where town property holders paid an "annual and perpetual" rent to the congregation of St. Martin of Tours Catholic Church.

ST. MAURICE (Winn Parish)   *District 8, across river from Natchitoches*
St. Maurice Plantation

Site of original land grant to Ignatio Sequin. Built in 1826 by Dennis Fort. Owned by William Prothro family, 1846–1856. Purchased by Dr. David H. Boullt in 1856. Later owned by E. W. Teddlie family. Restored in 1871.

STONEWALL (DeSoto Parish)   *District 4, Land's End Plantation*
Land's End Plantation—1835

Established by Colonel Henry Marshall, signer Louisiana Ordinance of Secession and Confederate Constitution, Member of Confederate Congress. House built 1857. Used as hospital Battle of Mansfield, 1864.

SULPHUR (Calcasieu Parish)   *US 90, District 7, west of town*
Sulphur Mines—One Mile North

In 1894 Herman Frasch, using process for first time, forced steam into salt dome caprock, returning solid molten sulphur to surface. Sicily sulphur monopoly was broken.

SUPREME (Assumption Parish)   *SH 1, District 61, in town*
Bayou Lafourche

Some early sources indicate that "River of the Washas" or "the west fork" was explored by Bienville (fall 1699) from the Mississippi to Washa (Ouacha) Indian village near here. Later the French would call the bayou "Lafourche (fork) of the Chitimachas," then Bayou Lafourche.

TANGIPAHOA (Tangipahoa Parish)   *US 51, District 62, in town*
Camp Moore

One of the principal Louisiana Confederate induction centers and training camps during the War for Southern Independence. Named for Governor Thomas Overton Moore. Over 400 soldiers buried in the camp cemetery.

TANGIPAHOA (Tangipahoa Parish)   *District 62, in town*
Tangipahoa

Area settled in early 1800s. New Orleans, Jackson & Great Northern Railroad built station here c. 1853. One square mile town formed around it in 1866. Included part of former Confederate Camp Moore. Town named for Indian tribe.

TANGIPAHOA (Tangipahoa Parish)   *District 62,*
Tourist Reception Center
Thirty-first Parallel

N. boundary of Tangipahoa Parish. Line established by Pinckney Treaty, Oct. 27, 1795, dividing southern United States and Spanish West Florida. Recognized U.S. claim dating back to American Revolution, 1783.

THIBODAUX (Lafourche Parish) *District 2, in town*
City of Thibodaux
Incorporated as a town on March 10, 1838. Early records show settlement existed in late 1790s as an important trading post for the Lafourche country. Named for Henri Schuyler Thibodaux (1769–1827), who gave the first land for the early village.

THIBODAUX (Lafourche Parish) *SH 1, District 2, in town*
Francis Tillou Nicholls
(1834–1912)
Homesite of distinguished Confederate brigadier-general, twice governor of Louisiana 1877–80 and 1888–92; he was appointed Chief Justice of the Louisiana State Supreme Court, serving from 1892–1911.

THIBODAUX (Lafourche Parish) *SH 20, District 2, in town*
St. John's Episcopal Church
One of the oldest Episcopal churches in the Mississippi Valley. St. John's Parish organized February, 1843. Cornerstone of church laid January 1844. Church consecrated March 1844 by Bishop Leonidas Polk, first Episcopal Bishop of Louisiana.

THIBODAUX (Terrebonne Parish) *Schriever Hwy., District 2*
Tomb of Henry Schuyler Thibodaux
Born Albany, New York, 1769. Died at his plantation near this place, 1827. "Father of Terrebonne Parish" and Acting Governor of Louisiana, 1824.

TUNICA (West Feliciana Parish) *District 61, in town*
Houmas Landing—Portage of the Cross
Near this site Houmas Village was visited by Henri de Tonti, 1686, by Iberville and party March 20, 1699. A chapel was built by Father Du Ru, a mission founded by Father de Limoges, 1700. As Tunica Indians took over the area, Houmas moved by 1709.

VACHERIE (St. James Parish)   *SH 18, District 2, in town*
Bayougoula Village, 1713

Settled by Canadians and French; later by Germans, Acadians, Spaniards. Here in 1730 Governor Perier organized expedition against Natchez Indians. Early cattle raising center. French records referred to area as Tabiscana.

VACHERIE (St. James Parish)   *SH 18, District 2, in town*
Colonel Leopold L. Armant

Enlisted in Confederate Army, 1861; died heroically at Battle of Mansfield, 1864. Served in Yellow Jacket Bat. Com. of 18th Vol. Inf. Reg. and Mouton Brig. His ancestors were Jean Marie, Jean Baptiste, and Jean Seraphim Armant, St. James planters and army officers.

VACHERIE (St. James Parish)   *SH 20, District 2, near Chegby*
Le Chemin Militaire

Route used by Civil War troops. It led from Mississippi river over swamp ridges, Indian trails, through Chackbay (Chegby), Thibodaux and Bayou Lafourche areas, Schriever, Gibson, Morgan city, to Attakapas country. Local militia units took active parts in Civil War engagements.

VACHERIE (St. James Parish)   *SH 18, District 2, in town*
"Le Petit Versailles"

Once famed plantation home and gardens of Valcour Aime 1798–1867. Birthplace Marie Francois Alcee Fortier, grandson and historian 1856–1914. 1768 La Vacherie of DeNoyan Brothers. Bienville's Grandnephews of Blanpain, Ranson, Jacquelin 1740–50s.

VACHERIE (St. James Parish)   *River Road, District 61, near town*
Oak Alley Plantation

Built (1837–39) by Jacques T. Roman, this fine example of Greek Revival architecture is famous for its alley of 28 evenly spaced live oak trees, believed to be at least 100 years older than "Big House." A NATIONAL HISTORIC LANDMARK.

VENICE (Plaquemines Parish)   *SH 23, District 2*

Fort Jackson

Built 1822–32 to protect the lower river. Named for Andrew Jackson. 1862—Fort withstood 10-day seige by Farragut and surrendered after city fell. In 1898 and 1917–18 used as training base. 1961—Fort was declared a national monument.

VENICE (Plaquemines Parish)   *SH 23, District 2, in town*

Venice

Near this site on April 9, 1682, LaSalle claimed Louisiana for France. Father Zenobius Membre, a member of the expedition, sang the *Te Deum.* On March 3, 1699, Father Anastase Douay, a member of Iberville's expedition, celebrated the first mass of record in French Louisiana.

VIDALIA (Concordia Parish)   *US 65/84, District 58,in town*

Sand Bar Fight

James Bowie, wounded as a second in Wells-Maddox duel and wielding the awesome blade of his design, killed Norris Wright Sept. 19, 1827. Modified knife later became famous as "The Bowie Knife."

VIENNA (Lincoln Parish)   *District 5, in town*

Vienna (Wire Road)

First called Colvin's Post-office in 1838, Vienna was incorporated in 1848. It was an overnight stop on the Trenton-Shreveport Stage Road, later called the "Wire Road" when the telegraph line was strung along it.

VILLE PLATTE (Evangeline Parish)   *SH 167, District 7,*
in front of City Hall

Ville Platte

Area first settled in late eighteenth century. Located on Spanish Royal Road. Marcellin Garand, former adjutant major in French army, regarded as founder. Incorporated in 1858. Parish seat of Evangeline Parish.

WALKER (Livingston Parish)
District 62, in front of town hall

Walker, Louisiana

Originally named Milton Old Field for Michael Milton who claimed land in 1853. Walker post office established in 1856. Named for Wm. E. Walker, M.D., state legislator and organizer of Co. D 16th LA Inf., CSA. Town incorporated in 1909.

Sponsored by Edward Livingston Historical Association, Inc.

WASHINGTON (St. Landry Parish)
SH 10, District 2, in town

Washington

Prosperous antebellum inland port and Western frontier gateway. Texas stage and river pakets interchanged passengers and mail. Passengers, freight were transferred to northbound craft.

WELCH (Jefferson Davis Parish)
US 90, District 7, in town

Early Cattle Industry

Long-horned Spanish cattle introduced by Avoyelles Indians long before the French arrived on the scene; used as foundation stock by pioneers. Acadians and other settled area, 1760s; developed vacheries (cattle ranches) in this prairie region of southwest La.

WEST FELICIANA (West Feliciana Parish)
In town

West Feliciana Railroad

One of South's earliest railroads. Ran from St. Francisville, La., to Woodville, Ms. Idea conceived in 1828 as means of transporting cotton to river. Chartered in 1831. Completed in 1842. In use in Illinois Central System until abandoned in 1978.

WEST MONROE (Ouachita Parish)
District 5,
Mt. Vernon Baptist Church

Old Fenner Road

Surveyed about 1830 by John, James, Richard, and Sherod, sons of William Fenner. In 1837 Mr. Vernon church built on road, which ran from the junction of Cheniere Creek and Ouachita River west to Okaloosa over Indian trails.

WEST MONROE (Ouachita Parish) *District 5, in town*
Olinkraft

First pulp paper mill in the United States to produce fourdrinier kraft liner-board. Was first hundred percent sulphate board on market. Produced in 1925.

WEST MONROE (Ouachita Parish) *District 5, in town*
Site of Filhiol House

In 1795 Don Juan Filhiol, commandant of Spanish Fort Miro, built a log cabin at what is now the corner of South Second and Colemen Streets. This was one of the first buildings in what is now West Monroe.

WEST MONROE (Ouachita Parish) *District 5, Trenton and Claiborne sts.*
Trenton

The first steamboat came into this area in 1819. Soon after, Trenton became the most important cotton shipping center on the Ouachita River. It was incorporated in 1870. It lost its importance soon after the railroad bridge across the River at Monroe went into service in 1882.

WINNFIELD (Winn Parish) *Long Home Site, District 8*
Huey Pierce Long, Sr., and Caledonia Tison Long

Birthplace of U.S. Senator Huey Pierce Long, Governor George Kemp Long, Congressman Shannon Long. This park site donated to the State of Louisiana by Earl K. Long and his wife Blanche Revere Long in loving memory of his mother and father, Caledonia Tison Long and Huey Pierce Long, Senator. It was his request that he be buried here at his birthplace near the home that he loved.

ZEMURRAY GARDENS (Tangipahoa Parish) *In town*
Zemurray Gardens Lodge

Joiner family settled here c. 1800. Later called Mount Hennen, Morris Retreat, Houltonwood. The Sam Zemurrays created gardens in 1930s aided by gardener Howard Schilling. Property acquired by Reimers-Schneider Trust, 1974.

Sponsored by Reimers-Schneider Trust.

ZWOLLE (Sabine Parish) *District 8, 1 mile south of town*
Early Spanish Missions

Catholic mission church built at Las Cabezas on Bayou Scie about 1795. Succeeded by Nuestra Senora de Guadalupe (Our Lady of Guadalupe). In 1858 referred to as St. Michael (San Miguel). Zwolle's St. Joseph's succeeds these.

ZWOLLE (Sabine Parish) *District 8, in front of church*
St. Joseph Catholic Church

Formerly a mission of Natchitoches, Nacogdoches, and Many, St. Joseph's has records by the first resident pastor, Fr. J.M. Ledreaux, dated 1881. Land was later obtained from John Sharnac (Ezernack) & Alex Cortinez.

Sponsored by St. Joseph Catholic Church of Zwolle.

About Louisiana African-American
Heritage Sites . . .

Louisiana's rich African-American heritage can be seen and celebrated throughout the state. The 34 sites within this section have been officially designated by the United States Department of Interior's National Park Service and are listed on the National Register of Historic Places. They pay tribute to literary figures and plantation owners, churches and chapels, schools and hospitals, accomplishment and determination. You'll visit slave cabins, Creole-owned plantations, sharecropping complexes, a Louisiana Native Guard battlefield, and surviving examples of a rare wooden cotton press, brick privy, and brick smokehouse. You'll glide through typical working-class neighborhoods and a one-time red light district. You'll feel the exotic pulse of Congo Square—site of the legendary Sunday slave dances—and the Roof Garden, a dance hall that wailed all night to the sounds of notables such as Duke Ellington, Louis Armstrong, and Fats Waller.

The information in this section has been culled almost verbatim from each site's statement of significance for the National Register of Historic Places nomination form, as written and compiled by the State of Louisiana Division of Historic Preservation.

ALEXANDRIA (Rapides Parish) *1327 Third St., in town*
Bontemps, Arna Wendell, House

The Arna Wendell Bontemps House is of national significance in the area of literature because it was the home of one of the most productive and versatile African-American writers of the twentieth century. Bontemps lived in the house from his birth in 1902 until 1906, when his family moved to California. Although a childhood home rather than one associated with Bontemps' productive life, the house is eligible for the Register because, according to scholars, the author's works were influenced greatly by this early, formative period. Also, the home was especially important to Bontemps, as evidenced by his words and actions and the reminiscences of his family. Finally, it could well be argued that Bontemps' childhood home is the most appropriate surviving resource to represent him.

Although far from a household word, Arna Bontemps' name is well known to scholars and students of African-American literature. Hence this nomination will provide only a summation of his life and career. Bontemps was born in 1902 to a middle-class Alexandria family. His father was a brickmason, his mother a teacher. As Bontemps later wrote: "Mine had not been a varmint-infested childhood so often the hallmark of Negro American autobiography. My parents and grandparents had been well-fed, well-clothed, and well-housed. . . ."

Bontemps' seemingly idyllic childhood in Central Lousiana, as described in his autobiographical essay "Why I Returned," ended when he was four. Because of a racial slur directed at his father, and more importantly, its larger implications, the family moved to California. Bontemps writes that the decision his father made as he walked home after the incident "changed everything for all of us."

After receiving his bachelor's degree in California in 1923, Bontemps accepted a teaching position at the Harlem Academy in New York, where he remained until 1931. There he became part of a reawakening in black culture known as the Harlem Renaissance. In 1924, his poetry first appeared in *Crisis* magazine, the NAACP periodical edited by Dr. W. E. B. DuBois, and three years later, he was awarded the publication's Poetry Prize. He also won the Alexander Pushkin Poetry Prize in 1926 and '27. His first novel, *God Sends Sunday,* was published in 1931. From 1931 to 1934, Bontemps taught in Huntsville, Alabama, and from '35 to '37 in Chicago. Upon completion of his master's degree in library science from the University of Chicago in 1943, he became head librarian at Fisk University in Nashville, a position he held until 1965. The eight years remaining in his life were spent as a professor at the University of Illinois at Chicago Circle and Yale, and finally as writer-in-residence at Fisk. He died at his Nashville home June 4, 1973.

Bontemps is known for the volume of his work and his versatility. He is the author of twenty-five books, including novels, children's books, biographies, histories, and collections of poems, and a handful of plays, some in collaboration with Countee Cullen. In addition, he served as editor or co-editor of various anthologies (for example, with Langston Hughes on *The Poetry of the Negro*).

Although Bontemps was quite young when he left Alexandria, he had definite memories of his childhood in the house under consideration, as affectionately recalled in his autobiographical essay "Why I Returned." His precocious childhood memories were reinforced and augmented by stories from relatives who also migrated to California from Central Louisiana. According to Bontemps, they were forever talking about things "back home."

By definition, a writer's work has elements of the autobiographical in it, and scholars note that this is particularly true of Bontemps, with Central Louisiana figuring prominently. According to Professor Charles L. James, who is presently working on a biography of the author, Central Louisiana represents "the central matrix" for his "fictive imagination." "It was the place of precocious childhood memory, the focal point of return when he spoke and wrote wistfully of his Southern past." Phyllis R. Klotman, Professor of Afro-American Studies at Indiana University, emphasizes how important a writer's early experiences are to later works. She writes: "Bontemps' writing especially is rooted to the past, to Alexandria his home, to Louisiana, and to the South." After visiting Alexandria for a Bontemps symposium, Professor Klotman noted: "The vivid descriptions of place in the short stories I first taught in the '70s assumed a reality for me that they had never had before."

It is clear that the house was special to Bontemps. As has been mentioned, he wrote fondly of his Alexandria childhood in his autobiographical essay, referring specifically to the house. By that time, 1965, he had been back to see it because he mentioned that the last time he visited Louisiana, the house in which he was born was freshly painted. His son, Arna Alexander Bontemps, notes that to his father "back home" always meant the house in Alexandria. The week before he died he had made arrangements to go home again to complete research he was doing for his autobiography and to take his sons to, in his words, "have another look at their grandparents' stomping ground."

Bontemps' widow and biographer Charles L. James feel unequivocally that the author's childhood home in Alexandria should be the resource to represent him in the National Register of Historic Places. According to them, the only other surviving building with any compelling association is his home in Nashville, which is non-historic (late '50s). In endorsing the National Register effort for her husband's childhood home, Mrs. Bontemps stated: "It's his roots. He started there; it's the place he wrote about." She continued that "no place should hold precedence over that place."

ALEXANDRIA (Rapides Parish) *Off US 71, about 6 miles south of town*
Inglewood Plantation Historic District

Inglewood Plantation is of state significance in the area of agriculture because it is one of Louisiana's most important surviving cotton plantation complexes. It is one of a very limited number of surviving complexes, and among these it is significant because of its size and the rarity of some of the individual structures.

The plantation system which dominated Louisiana's cotton-growing parishes was initially characterized by slave labor controlled by a centralized overseer or planter. After the Civil War, the prevailing system shifted to sharecropping, wherein an individual farmer worked a tract of plantation land in return for a share of the crop. Often, the farmer's share was placed under a crop-lien mortgage as security for credit purchases of food and supplies. Because of this lien, relatively few sharecroppers cleared more than $20 or so a year in profit. But despite its drawbacks, sharecropping actually bolstered the state's plantation system, albeit in a modified form. For example, in 1900 there were more plantations and fewer small farms than there were in 1860. Although the sharecropping system persisted well into the twentieth century, Inglewood shifted to centralized farming using a manager and paid labor after 1900.

In the historic period, well over a third of Louisiana's parishes were devoted to cotton production, but little remains to represent the overall rural landscape that this created. Today, cotton farming is largely mechanized, with massive machines housed under enormous metal canopies. Gone are the quarters houses, the mule barns, the old plantation stores, and the coterie of other support structures. A fair number of plantation houses remain in the cotton-growing parishes, but relatively few retain any historic dependencies. Fewer still are parts of sizable agricultural complexes with ten or more buildings. Inglewood contains a total of twenty-one contributing support buildings which span the entire historic plantation period. There are probably only a handful of cotton complexes of comparable size and quality. Inglewood contains four barns and nine quarters houses, which is a larger number in each case than one usually finds, if indeed one finds any at all. Moreover, it retains an extremely rare example of a sharecropping cotton house. It also contains what is thought to be the cotton region's only pre-1900 brick privy and a very rare brick smokehouse. Finally, its commissary and office is of brick, which is unusual.

BAKER (East Baton Rouge Parish) *Near town, off Groom Road, 1 mile west of SH 19*

Leland College

The extant buildings on the Leland College campus are historically significant on the state level in the areas of education and black history because they are the only remaining visual reminders of a black educational institution of statewide importance. Although the school operated for forty-five years in New Orleans, there are no extant structures there associated with it. The nominated buildings on the Baker campus are the only structures left to represent the history of the institution.

Leland College (originally Leland University) had a far-reaching impact upon the education of Louisiana blacks. It was one of four institutions of higher learning for blacks chartered in the state either during or shortly after Reconstruction. The other three were Southern University (1880), Straight University (1869), and New Orleans University (1873). Southern began in New Orleans and moved to Baton Rouge in 1914, while the latter two were in New Orleans for their existence. In 1935 they merged to form Dillard University. It should be noted that although all of these institutions were called universities and are thought of as such, none of them during the period under consideration (1870–1930) had more than a small percentage of students enrolled in what could be considered college-level courses. The vast majority of their enrollees were elementary and secondary students.

In addition to these four schools, there were two black institutions of higher learning which have their roots in the early twentieth century. Xavier University began at the old Southern campus in New Orleans and purchased its present site in June of 1929. Present-day Grambling University began as a private industrial school on the elementary and secondary levels. It did not begin to award college degrees until 1944.

During the course of its history, Leland College educated thousands of black Louisianians. Its main efforts were directed toward training educators and ministers. Leland alumni took jobs as teachers, principals, and pastors throughout the state, thereby extending the institution's influence even further. Some of these individuals rose to positions of leadership within their professions and the black community. For example, Southern University owes much to Leland graduate Joseph Samuel Clark, its president during the crucial period following its relocation in Baton Rouge. (Clark was president from 1914–1938.)

Finally, Leland had increased statewide impact because of its system of preparatory "feeder" schools. It exercised an influence on various upper elementary and secondary schools by allowing them to become Leland auxiliaries. Faculty and curricula selection at these affiliates was supervised by Leland. In fact, faculty members at auxiliaries were considered to be part of the Leland faculty, and their salaries were paid by the parent institution. The affiliates had to pay Leland tuition for each enrollee. Graduates of these schools were accepted into Leland without examination and good students were awarded small scholarships. The 1909–1910 Leland bulletin lists ten such schools in locations throughout the state.

It is important to note that although a total of six black "colleges" or "universities" operated in Louisiana from c. 1870 to c. 1930, there is very little left as a visual reminder of these institutions. There is nothing left of the old Leland campus in New Orleans. Nor is there anything left of the New Orleans campuses of Southern university, Straight University, or New Orleans University. As far as can be determined, the oldest structure on the Xavier campus is the administration building, which dates from 1930 or 1931. The oldest buildings at Grambling appear to date from the 1930s and the overall impression is that of a modern campus. Only Southern University in Baton Rouge and Leland College in Baker have significant collections of pre-1930 educational structures. Thus, the Leland campus constitutes one of two extant collections of buildings which, to a large extent, represent the whole of black higher education during the period under consideration (1870–1930).

BATON ROUGE (East Baton Rouge Parish) *District 6, 1500 East Blvd.*
McKinley High School

The McKinley High School Building is locally significant because of the role it has played in the education of blacks in the Baton Rouge area. Prior to its construction in 1926 and opening in September 1927, the only place area blacks could receive a secondary education was at a joint elementary-high school named Baton Rouge High School (1914–1927). When McKinley was completed, the high school program of this school was phased out. Thus, the McKinley High School was the first school in Baton Rouge constructed solely for the purpose of providing a high school education for area blacks. For many years it served as the only secondary educational facility for blacks within a 40-mile radius of Baton Rouge.

McKinley High School was converted to a junior high school in 1949 when a new high school was constructed on McCalop Street. In 1956 McKinley became an elementary school and then was phased out as a school in 1972. Since that time it has been used by various community groups such as the South Baton Rouge Community Action Service, the South Baton Rouge Health Referral Center, and the South Baton Rouge Head Start Center.

McKinley High School is also significant in the area of architecture as an unusually pretentious black secondary school. Other examples across the state are typically much humbler structures. Most were frame rather than brick, and most had little or no ornamentation. In addition, the building is a local landmark in the South Baton Rouge-upper Highland Road area, most of which has a residential scale.

BATON ROUGE (East Baton Rouge Parish) *1335 North Blvd., in town*
Prince Hall Masonic Temple

The Prince Hall Masonic Temple is locally significant in the area of entertainment/recreation because it housed two facilities, the Temple Theatre and the Temple Roof Garden, which were entertainment focal points for black Baton Rougeans. The period of significance spans from 1924, the date of construction, to 1944, the fifty-year cutoff. The theatre and ballroom continued to play important roles into the post-World War II era.

At one time or another during the historic period, there were three theatres in Baton Rouge for the city's large black population: the Grand, which according to city directories closed c. 1936; McKinley Theatre, which first appears in the 1936 city directory; and the Temple Theatre, which operated from the building's construction into the post-war era. Of these, only the Temple survives. Of course, in the pre-television era, movie theatres were major sources of entertainment. The Temple attracted patrons from not only Baton Rouge, but nearby Scotlandville, where Southern University, a black institution, is located. According to individuals interviewed for this nomination, there was no theatre in Scotlandville during the historic period. In addition to movies, the Temple also hosted vaudeville acts.

The Temple's legendary claim to fame in Baton Rouge's black community is the Temple Roof Garden. Stories about dances held in the ballroom are legion. Apparently its heyday as the place to go was in the late 1930s and 1940s. It was particularly popular among youth clubs for dances. Interviewees recall hiring a band when they were flush, or when times were tight, paying someone to "spin" records. However, it was the "big name" bands brought to the Temple Roof Garden by the management that fill the memories of black Baton Rougeans, who reminisce about hundreds of people dancing the night away to the sounds of such well-known bands and entertainers as Fats Waller, Duke Ellington, Louis Armstrong, Cab Calloway, and the like. An ad appearing in January 1938 proclaimed the Temple Roof Garden the "finest dancing hall South." A headline in the same issue of *The Baton Rouge Post* read "Harlem Play Girls Swing Before a Record Crowd." "It was a gay night for all on the beautiful Temple Roof Garden," wrote the reporter. Like the theatre, the ballroom drew its patrons from Baton Rouge and nearby Southern University. According to interviewees, there were no other comparable facilities in the city available to blacks during the historic period.

BATON ROUGE (East Baton Rouge Parish)   *In town, 900 North 19th St.*
Scott Street School

The Scott Street School is locally significant in the areas of education and ethnic history because it represents the "coming of age" of the effort to provide public-funded education for the African-American children of Baton Rouge.

Like the rest of the South, Louisiana was slow to make free public education available to African-American children after the Civil War. In Baton Rouge, the first serious efforts to educate these children were made by local churches. The two black Methodist congregations cooperated to establish a school known as the Hamilton Academy. The Baptists consolidated classes previously offered in their churches into a private secondary school known as the Baton Rouge Academy. The latter facility operated between 1875 and 1916 and provided elementary and secondary education. In addition, it offered the only teacher training course for blacks outside of New Orleans. Both of these private schools seem to have had adequate facilities and equipment, and both were strongly supported by the black community. A third institution, known as the Live Oak School, was also founded during the

Reconstruction period. It was operated by a white missionary from New York State and eventually became an orphanage for black children.

Public records for the Reconstruction era are sparse, and the few early records which survive do not differentiate between the races. Therefore, it is difficult to determine the availability or quality of public education available to African-American children in Baton Rouge before 1877. In that year, the parish school board identified several possible locations for black schools, but it appears that only two were actually placed in service. Both schools apparently made use of already existing structures such as residences, churches, or lodge halls, for no special buildings were constructed to house them. By 1891, these two schools had combined and were holding classes in a small, two-story building on Hickory Street. A future black educator who saw the building in 1908 described it as ". . . a very unattractive, unpainted, (unceiled and unpartitioned frame) building . . . with space enough for the small number of children in attendance, but ill-adapted in every way to the purpose intended." According to this witness, for many years the parish school board failed to approve any expenditure of public funds to provide the black children of the city with such bare necessities as pure drinking water, sanitary toilets, and proper heating and ventilating facilities. Nevertheless, for twenty-three years this inadequate building served as the only public institution of learning for black children in the city.

Educational opportunities for black children began to improve with the appointment of H. M. Strickland as parish school superintendent in 1905. Strickland soon raised the salaries of black teachers and fixed the length of the school term at nine months for city children and four months for rural residents. In 1908 he hired an entirely new and better trained teaching staff for the Hickory Street School, and hired an experienced principal as well. However, these improvements made no real impression upon the black community, which continued to send its children to the church-sponsored private schools.

Recognizing that black parents would not send their children to the public school until its physical condition was improved, Strickland and the principal persuaded the school board to appropriate $300 for improvements in 1908. This sum funded exterior painting and the construction of partitions to form separate classrooms. A short time later, a friend of the school collected $50 and hired a plumber to connect the building with the city's water supply. Thereafter, attendance at the Hickory Street School increased so much that both the building and the teaching staff had to be expanded the next year.

Further progress in black education was made in 1913, when Baton Rouge Mayor Jules Roux promised to expand and improve the African-American school in return for the black community's support in an upcoming bond election. Eventually a request for $25,000 for a new black school building was placed on the ballot. The proposal carried easily and marked a significant change on the part of both the white and African-American communities with regard to supporting black education. With the money thus raised, the city built its first modern brick school for black children. In fact, the building was the first modern school to be erected for black children at public expense in the State of Louisiana. The black community's acceptance of the new school was overwhelming, and within three years' time an additional facility was needed. Baton Rouge voters approved funds for a second African-American school (the Reddy Street School) in 1916 and a third (the Scott Street School) in 1920. The latter, built in 1922, had fourteen classrooms, a library, principal's office, restroom, and other modern conveniences. These three modern schools represented a "coming of age" for black education in Baton Rouge because, in addition to providing better physical facilities and space for more students, they allowed teachers to separate students by age and grade. Unfortunately, the first two modern schools did not survive. Thus, the Scott Street School is the only surviving symbol of this important "coming of age" and is an outstanding candidate for National Register listing.

BERMUDA (Natchitoches Parish)   *District 5, near town, at end of dirt road off SH 494, about 1 mile northwest of town*

Maison de Marie Therese

The Maison de Marie Therese is architecturally significant as an early and well-preserved example of a Creole raised cottage. This can be seen in its plan, its moldings and chairrails, its hewn timbers and panelled bousillage. Perhaps the complex and untypical roof structure was the result of untrained builders, who were used to pitched roofs but were faced with the problem of constructing a hip roof. Perhaps it simply reflects a total lack of understanding of structures on the part of slave builders. Whatever the reason for its existence, it is very probably unique in Natchitoches Parish. Crude and inept, its overstructuring gives strong evidence of an unsophisticated building technology and represents an inherent part of the early architectural development of the area.

The house is also significant in the area of black history as the home of Marie Therese Coincoin (1742–1816?), a remarkable black woman whose achievements were the foundation of the network of plantations owned by the Cane River region's famous "Creoles of color."

It is not absolutely certain that the house was lived in by Marie Therese or that it dates from the time of her occupation of the site. But, as Dr. Carolyn French, one of several scholars who has done research on the house, notes, ". . . the evidence is overwhelming that this is the former home of Marie Therese" . . . Both French and Gary Mills point out that the building is located on the site designated as a land grant to Marie Therese by a survey plat of 1794. In addition, there is a building indicated on the plat map and labeled "Maison de Marie Therese, Negresse libre" (see . . . Dr. French's letter noted above; and Mill's article "Historian Responds to Story About Marie Therese," *Natchitoches Times,* 4 May 1978).

Louis Nardini, who did historical research on this site in 1972, reported that the land was given to Marie Therese in 1786 and that she had resided on the land from 1778. (Nardini's report is in the possession of Mr. and Mrs. John E. Prudhomme, former owners of the house.) In addition, Dr. H. F. Gregory has done some archaeological research on the site. He reported, "My impression is that the occupation of the site, and likely the house . . . began about 1770–80. It appears to have been continuously occupied since that date." He also noted that his findings correlate well with the historical documents concerning the land and with the "architectural and hardware features of the house" (see letter from Dr. Gregory to Dr. Whittington, 1 November 1978, copy in Maison de Marie de Therese file). The evidence for Marie Therese's residence in the house is therefore strong.

Marie Therese Coincoin was born a slave of Louis Juchereau de St. Denis, the founder of Natchitoches. He died in 1744, but she remained the slave of his family until 1778. At this time she was purchased and freed by Claude Thomas Pierre Metoyer, a Frenchman who had settled in Natchitoches. She had borne several children by him during the previous decade. Marie Therese remained his mistress until 1786, when they ended their alliance and he gave her the land which is the site of the Maison de Marie Therese.

She began to operate a small plantation on this land and worked to free several of her children and grandchildren who were still in slavery. From then on to her death in 1816 or 1817, she expanded her landholdings and gradually achieved the manumission of her children and grandchildren. With her death, she left her descendants what Mills calls a "comfortable" estate, consisting of at least sixteen slaves and over a thousand arpents of land. Contrary to legend, she did not leave behind a fabulous amount of wealth. Her foremost legacy, according to Mills, was her example of determination, industry, frugality, mutual assistance, and emphasis upon working with the white people rather than against them to achieve one's goal.

Her sons and daughters of mixed blood were able to expand the property she left into the vast, rich plantations which they came to own on Cane River. Among these was the plantation now known as Melrose, which became the center of their holdings. Their sizable domain began with the land that is the site of the house in which Marie Therese Coincoin apparently lived in the early years of her freedom. (The foregoing biographical sketch of Marie Therese is based on Gary B. Mills, *The Forgotten People: Cane River's Creoles of Color,* Baton Rouge: LSU Press, 1977, pp. 1–49.)

BUNKIE (Avoyelles Parish)   *US 71, in town*
Edwin Epps House

The Edwin Epps House is of national significance in the areas of literature and social/humanitarian because of its close association with the famous slave narrative *Twelve Years A Slave.* Epps was Northup's master for the last ten years of his twelve-year enslavement, and the Epps House figures very prominently in *Twelve Years A Slave.*

Twelve Years A Slave is the extraordinary story of Solomon Northup, a free black adult from New York who was kidnapped and enslaved in Louisiana. It was first published in 1853, shortly after Northup's rescue, under the title *Twelve Years a Slave, Narrative of Solomon Northup, a Citizen of New York, Kidnapped in Washington City in 1841, and Rescued in 1853 from a Cotton Plantation Near the Red River in Louisiana.*

Northup was reunited with his family in Glen Falls, New York on January 20, 1853, and shortly thereafter began work on the narrative with the aid of a local writer named David Wilson. The book was actually written by Wilson, but as dictated to him by Northup. Unlike most of the ghost writers of slave narratives, Wilson was not an antislavery activist. Historians Sue Eakin and Joseph Logsdon, the editors of the most recent edition of *Twelve Years A Slave,* theorize that Wilson "merely became intrigued with the tragedy and recognized its publishing potential." They also feel there is no reason to doubt Wilson's statement, made in the original preface to the book, that he had dedicated himself to an accurate transcription of Northup's reminiscences.

Slave narratives were immensely popular reading in the North, and *Twelve Years A Slave* was certainly no exception. Its sensational element (i.e., a free black kidnapped and sold into slavery) made it a best seller of its genre. The narrative was an immediate success; the first printing of 8,000 copies was sold within a month. It sold over 30,000 copies in American and European editions during Northup's lifetime and was reprinted several times after his death in 1863. In addition, his story received considerable publicity from articles in Northern newspapers as well as in the antislavery press.

Not only did Northup's story capture the general public's attention, but it also merited comment from such well-known figures as Harriet Beecher Stowe and Frederick Douglass. The first newspaper account of Northup's story (*New York Times,* January 19, 20, 1853) mentioned the similarity to *Uncle Tom's Cabin* and Stowe herself termed it a "striking parallel" to her novel. In *The Key to Uncle Tom's Cabin* (1853), she related Northup's story and noted "the singular coincidence that this man was carried to a plantation in the Red River country, that same region where the scene of Tom's captivity was laid." Frederick Douglass, who had already recounted his experiences as a slave, recognized the compounded tragedy in Northup's account: "Think of it: For thirty years a man, with all a man's hopes, fears and aspirations—with a wife and children to call him by the endearing names of husband and father—with a home, humble it may be, but still a home . . . then for twelve years a thing, a chattel personal, classed with mules and horses . . . . Oh! It is horrible. It chills the blood to think that such are." (*Liberator,* August 26, 1853, quoted from *Frederick Douglass' Newspaper*).

Northup also apparently did some public speaking in the North on his experiences. A reaction to one such personal appearance can be found in a letter to William Lloyd Garrison two years after the first appearance of *Twelve Years A Slave:* "*Twelve Years A Slave* has been widely read in New England, and no narrative of man's experience as a slave . . . is more touching, or better calculated to expose the true character and designs of slaveholders. But it is far more potent to see the man, and hear him, in his clear, manly, straightforward way, speak of slavery as he experienced it, and as he saw it in others. Those who have read his Narrative can scarce fail to desire to see the man . . . and to hear his story from his own lips."

The Epps House figures very prominently in Northup's rescue, as described in the final portion of *Twelve Years A Slave*. In fact, it is the only extant structure directly associated with the narrative. As noted elsewhere, Epps was Northup's master for the last ten years of his enslavement.

"In the month of June, 1852, . . ." recounts Northup, "Mr. Avery, a carpenter of Bayou Rouge, commenced the erection of a house for Master Epps." Because of his skill as a carpenter, Northup was assigned to help with the building of the house, and it was thus he met Samuel Bass, the man most instrumental in his return to freedom. (Bass was one of the carpenters working on the house.) After overhearing Bass express antislavery sentiments to Epps, Northup decided to approach him for help. Northup explains that he waited until early August when he and Bass were alone working on the house to broach the subject. Bass was receptive and he met Northup that night in the unfinished house to hear the details of his story. Bass wrote letters to various Northern friends of Northup's, acquainting them with his situation, and seeking their assistance to secure his release. Because of the risk involved, Bass understandably remained anonymous. One of these letters reaped results when on January 3, 1853, Henry Northup, the scion of the family that had owned Northup's father, arrived at Epps' plantation to secure Northup's release. It was in the Epps House that Henry Northup and the local sheriff confronted Edwin Epps with Northup's true identity.

One wonders if Northup would have ever secured his freedom had it not been for the construction of this house. Would he have met Samuel Bass otherwise? Perhaps, but suffice it to say that Solomon Northup undoubtedly considered the construction of the house to be of special importance in ending his twelve years as a slave.

BURNSIDE (Ascension Parish)   *SH 75 and SH 44, near town*
St. Joseph's School

St. Joseph's School is of local significance in the area of education as a rare representation of the important role the Roman Catholic Church played in the education of blacks in rural southern Louisiana during the late nineteenth and early twentieth centuries.

In 1866, Roman Catholic bishops, convening in plenary council in Baltimore, decreed that every effort should be made to establish Catholic schools for the newly freed black children. The following year, St. Joseph's was established in Convent as the first black Catholic school in Louisiana. The school was staffed and administered by the Religious of the Sacred Heart and was located on the Sacred Heart Academy property. As previously mentioned, the original building was destroyed in 1890, and the present building was built in 1892. Between 1892 and the move to St. Michael's Church in 1932, St. Joseph's enrolled about 90 students annually, dispensing a high-quality elementary education. A student was given a "credit card" upon graduation which could be used to obtain admission to various black Catholic high schools in New Orleans.

It should be emphasized that, to a very large extent, black Catholic schools such as St. Joseph's were the only places where blacks could receive high-quality, consistent elementary education in rural southern Louisiana. Although there were other educational opportunities available, they were either of poor quality or of tenuous existence. The home school, where a mother taught groups of neighborhood children, was one alternative to black Catholic education. But these only existed sporadically, instruction was not consistent, and the teachers were often poorly educated themselves.

The other alternative was the state-supported school system, such as it was. After Reconstruction, a legislative act provided for a system of separate "public" education for blacks and whites. This was, in effect, more a quasi-public effort because the state provided only some of the funding, with local sources providing the building and other necessities. The schools were usually located in churches or lodge buildings, and teachers were poorly qualified. With the retrenchment politics of the day and the general lack of interest in public education, funding was woefully inadequate for even a single-school system, let alone the dual system mandated by segregation. From the beginning, black schools were generally not treated equally in the distribution of funds, and received an increasingly disproportionate share as white schools grew in number and importance. Also, of course, the notion of educating blacks certainly ran contrary to the racial attitudes of the time.

Indeed, black "schools" were really not schools at all. Essentially meager public subsidies were used to support quasi-private efforts. As T. H. Harris, State Superintendent of Education from 1908 to 1940, reported in his autobiography: "In most cases Negro churches were used for schoolhouses and the only equipment in these churches were the benches used for church services. The school term was from two to four months and the teachers were uneducated and wholly unequipped to instruct children."

By contrast, the black Catholic schools provided good facilities with motivated teachers. They remained the one bright spot in black education in rural southern Louisiana until the coming of the philanthropic Julius Rosenwald schools in the 1920s. During the late nineteenth and early twentieth centuries, many Roman Catholic communities had black academies such as St. Joseph's. Although no survey has been done, it is reasonable to assume that almost all of the original buildings have been lost. Black academies were part of larger Roman Catholic school complexes and consequently have been subject to improvements, enlargements, and incorporation into larger frame buildings. As far as the State Historic Preservation office is aware, St. Joseph's is one of only two pre-Rosenwald era black Catholic schools remaining in rural southern Louisiana. It is therefore of great importance as a reminder of the historic role of the Roman Catholic Church in black education in the region.

DERRY (Natchitoches Parish)   *District 5, Cane River area*
Magnolia Plantation

Magnolia Plantation is significant primarily for its excellent complex of outbuildings and dependencies. The slave quarters show a degree of constructional quality and architectural refinement seldom seen in slave dwellings. Moreover, it is unusual for a plantation to retain any slave dwellings at all, and it is highly unusual for slave dwellings to survive in sufficient numbers to constitute a complex, as they do at Magnolia.

The c. 1830 wooden cotton press is truly of national significance as a representative of the cotton production technology of its period. There are probably only about five or six comparable examples in the South.

Magnolia Plantation is also significant because of its plantation house, one of the largest plantation houses in the area, albeit an undistinguished one.

The land which was to become the nucleus of Magnolia Plantation was obtained by Jean Baptiste Lecomte in a French grant of 1753 and by Ambrose Lecomte in a Spanish grant of 1787. Ambrose Lecomte II was the founder of Magnolia. Maps in the State Land Office made by surveyors in 1827 and 1844 designate Ambrose Lecomte as the owner of the nucleus of the plantation. It was about 1840, according to family tradition, when Ambrose Lecomte II built the home at Magnolia.

Census data from 1850 suggests that by that time he was prospering. In that year, Ambrose Lecomte was 42 years old and owner of 182 slaves and $125,000 worth of real estate. His wife Desiree was 32 years old, and with them in the household were four daughters and a son. In 1852, Matthew Hertzog, twenty-four-years-old, married Lecomte's twenty-one year old daughter Atala. Soon afterward, he assumed management of the plantation.

As of 1860, Lecomte was the largest slaveholder in Natchitoches Parish and the largest producer of cotton. He owned a total of 7,835 acres of land, of which 2,240 were improved. His 234 slaves lived in 70 slave dwellings. The previous year, his plantation had produced 1,133 bales (450-pound bales) of cotton and 20,000 bushels of Indian corn. He owned $190,915 worth of real estate and $257,050 worth of personal property.

The decade of the 1860s brought great changes at Magnolia. In 1864, after the Battles of Mansfield and Pleasant Hill, the army of Union General Banks retreated to Alexandria by way of the Cane River country. Some of the soldiers burned the home at Magnolia, killing the caretaker, according to family tradition, under the front steps. The family was not at the plantation, having moved temporarily to Natchitoches.

Apparently, Ambrose Lecomte II died some time during the decade of the 1860s, for his name does not appear in the 1870 census. The figures for Matthew Hertzog for that year suggest that the war and its aftermath had greatly reduced the family's holdings. After the war, with the "big house" gone, the family lived in the nearby overseer's house. In 1870, Hertzog owned 2,400 acres of land, of which 1,000 were improved. The value of his farm was $12,000 and of his livestock $8,190. The estimated value of his farm production of the previous year was $17,839. The farm had yielded 163 bales of cotton (450-pound bales), 3,000 bushels of corn, 420 pounds of wool, and 25 bushels of sweet potatoes. Matthew Hertzog was 41 years old, and listed the value of his real estate at $12,000 and of his personal estate at $8,390. With him in the household were his wife Atala, two daughters, and three black servants.

In 1899, the "big house" was restored, utilizing the original brick foundation and the surviving brick walls and brick pillars. Ownership of Magnolia Plantation has remained in the same family down to the present. Today it is being farmed in cotton, soy beans, and cattle.

DONALDSONVILLE (Ascension Parish)   *SH 405, three miles west in*
community of McCall

Evan Hall Slave Cabins

The Evan Hall Slave Cabins are of state significance in the area of architecture because they represent unusually fine surviving examples of a once common antebellum building type which has all but disappeared from the state.

The census schedules of 1860 reveal that there were approximately 1,640 holdings of 50 or more slaves in Louisiana on the eve of the Civil War. In addition, there were, of course, innumerable holdings of less than 50. This indicates that at one time there must easily have been thousands of slave cabins across the state. They were a very predominant feature of the rural landscape, vastly outnumbering the plantation houses. However, today this situation is reversed and antebellum plantation houses have survived in greater numbers than slave quarters. As far as the State Historic Preservation Office is aware, there are only eight collections of rural slave cabins remaining in Louisiana. This figure includes only those collections in their original locations. There are a few more small collections of frame slave cabins which were moved to their present locations from various places.

DORSEYVILLE (Iberville Parish)   *31925 Lacroix Rd.*
St. John Baptist Church

St. John Baptist Church is locally significant in the areas of ethnic heritage and exploration/settlement because it represents the earliest history of the African-American community of Dorseyville. The period of significance was chosen to represent the early history of the community. It spans from the construction of the church (c. 1871) to 1893, by which time Dorseyville had a school (see below).

Dorseyville takes its name from Reverend Bazile Dorsey, the first pastor of St. John Church and the recognized founder of the community. Surrounded by sugarcane plantations, the village developed in the years immediately following the Civil War as a place for black agricultural workers to live. According to a cornerstone on the church, St. John was organized in 1868 and incorporated September 19, 1869. "B. Dorsey" is also inscribed on the stone. Conveyance records show that the property was acquired on October 30, 1871. An October 23, 1875, purchase of additional land refers to the church as being built.

The community was sufficiently established to appear on Mississippi River Commission maps of 1879–80. Various buildings are shown in what is labeled "Dorcyville," and the village's present layout was in place (two long streets running perpendicular to the Mississippi River). In 1881, a post office was established at Dorseyville, remaining in operation through 1918. By 1893, local children had a school, thanks to the efforts of St. John Baptist Church under the leadership of Reverend Dorsey. In a public/private arrangement very typical of black education in Louisiana at the time, the church provided a building and the parish school board some financial support. The two-room school taught grades 1–7.

Unfortunately, little survives to represent the early history of Dorseyville. Although the school building is still there, it has been altered to such an extent that it would not be recognizable to someone from the historic period. Most of the residences are either modern or significantly altered older buildings. Surviving historic buildings include a small minority of homes (late nineteenth/early twentiety century) and St. John Baptist Church.

Although there is no written record of the founding of Dorseyville, it seems likely that it grew up around St. John's, given the early founding of the congregation and construction of the church building (i.e., just a few years after the end of the Civil War). Expressing the high aspirations of newly freed slaves and the pivotal role of the church in black culture, St. John is a large, rather pretentious building within its context. As a powerful visual reminder of Dorseyville's early history, it is an excellent candidate for the National Register.

FERRIDAY (Concordia Parish)   *SH 901, District 5,*
                                                    12 miles northeast of town

Canebrake

Canebrake Plantation is the most agriculturally significant antebellum plantation complex in Concordia Parish, Louisiana. This significance is based on the survival and integrity of the slave cabins located in the "quarter lot" behind the main house and on the importance of the main house as a rare surviving example of an overseer's house on a plantation owned and operated by an absentee landlord who belonged to the planting aristocracy of Natchez, Mississippi. By the early 19th century, Concordia Parish had become principally a planting province for the planters who resided in Natchez in grand townhouses or suburban villa residences. By 1860, over 81% of the parish land was owned by these absentee owners and 91% of the population consisted of slaves (D. Clayton James, *Antebellum Natchez* [Baton Rouge: Louisiana State University Press, 1968], p. 148).

The main house on Canebrake is a good example of a typical raised Louisiana cottage with wide-open central passage and was probably constructed c. 1840 while the plantation was owned by Tobias Gibson and his partner William Harris, a planter who resided at Ravenna in Natchez. The original small size and plain finishes of the house and its close proximity to the quarter lot denote the role of the house as an overseer's cottage rather than a resident planter's dwelling. Nevertheless, the overseer's cottage is held physically, thus socially, aloof from the slave cabins by its elevation on high brick foundation piers, by its position slightly removed and forward from the quarter lot, and by its higher degree of finish. Although enlarged twice, the architectural integrity of the house has been little compromised, since changes were in the form of additions rather than subtractions. The most unusual and well-detailed architectural feature of the house is the use of double-leaf, hinged doors to enclose the central passage. These doors were probably installed in the mid-19th century when Canebrake was owned by Gerard Brandon of Brandon Hall near Natchez. The five double slave cabins of the rear "quarter lot," their construction and their physical relationship to each other, the overseer's house, the barn, and the cotton fields provide a rare tangible resource for studying the living conditions of the slave and overseer of a large antebellum cotton plantation.

In 1910, Canebrake Plantation was purchased by Arthur Meserve of Illinois, whose grandson, Barry Maxwell, now resides in the main house. Unoccupied for a number of years, the house is being restored and renovated as a permanent family residence for the Maxwell family.

Canebrake is locally significant in the area of agriculture because it is a rare surviving example of the type of plantation complex which dominated the agricultural landscape of antebellum Concordia Parish. As described below, 81% of the parish's land was owned by absentee landowners who lived across the river in Natchez, Mississippi. Hence, a typical plantation complex in the parish consisted of what one finds at Canebrake—an overseer's house, slave cabins, and outbuildings. The context for evaluation is Concordia Parish. The complex is being nominated for significance on the local level.

In most of the antebellum South, agriculture and agricultural life centered around the plantations and the plantation houses. The rural landscape was divided into plantation fiefdoms, each of which was the center of its own little world. Each plantation was also an agricultural unit in which farming was administered by the local landowner who lived on the property.

Natchez, Mississippi, was one of a number of exceptions to this agricultural land pattern. The great planters of Natchez lived in a state of splendid absentee ownership in a manner similar to European aristocrats, albeit on a smaller scale. Although these planters owned land throughout much of southern Louisiana, their holdings were concentrated in neighboring Concordia Parish. For example, in 1860, they owned 81% of the land in the parish. To a large extent, Concordia Parish was farmed through the use of plantation complexes consisting of an overseer's house, slave quarters, and outbuildings, but with no main house as such. (No main house was needed because the master was not in residence.) Essentially these were agricultural colonies to Natchez. They were also the most important factor in the parish's antebellum agricultural development.

Although many of the grand houses of Natchez have been preserved, little remains of the plantation complexes in Concorida Parish which supported them. As far as the Louisiana State Historic Preservation Office is aware, Canebrake is the only surviving example of this type of farm complex in the parish. It is, therefore, a very important visual reminder of the parish's antebellum agricultural history. Canebrake takes on added significance when one considers that agriculture was by far the leading force in the development of Concordia Parish during the nineteenth century.

KENTWOOD (Tangipahoa Parish) *District 6, in town*
Old Dormitory of the Tangipahoa Parish Training School
Home Economics Building

The Old Dormitory of the Tangipahoa Parish Training School (one of the school's two oldest remaining buildings) is significant in the areas of education and black history due to its close association with the school. The Tangipahoa Parish Training School, founded in 1911, was the first "county training school" in the entire South. A "county training school" was conceived as the only school of its kind in each county or parish. It would be centrally located and would provide instruction for Negro children in grades one through ten (or eleven) with a stress on "vocational" and "industrial" education at the secondary level. It would also provide teacher training so that its graduates could staff the rural black schools in the parish. The "county training schools" were the real beginning of secondary public education for blacks in the rural South.

The most complete account of the establishment of the Tangipahoa Parish Training School is found in Edward E. Redcay, *County Training Schools and Public Secondary Education for Negroes in the South* (Washington, D.C.: The John F. Slater Fund, 1935, pp. 24–30). The initiative was taken in September, 1910, by Professor A. M. Strange, who had recently left Mississippi and moved to Kentwood. He wrote to Dr. James H. Dillard, general agent for the John F. Slater Fund (a philanthropic fund for the advancement of Negro education), soliciting aid for a black school that would be located in Kentwood. He wrote Dr. Dillard another letter in November, again soliciting aid and in the process revealing his conception of the school and telling of support in the Kentwood area for the school.

"We have succeeded in interesting the good white people of this section of parish and parish board of education to help us put the before mentioned idea into execution. This school fosters the idea of having boys learn scientific agriculture, dairying and horticulture for girls sewing, domestic economy, cooking, dairying and poultry raising. We have cleaned up 10 acres and will soon begin fencing. We need at least $4000.00 to finish our building and get in running order. We therefore ask you as a conservative southern gentleman, to help us in this movement, the best and conservative white ladies and gentlemen of this section are doing everything to make movement succeed. The mills have donated lumber, brickyard brick, the Negro laborers at the mills have signed petition to give $.25 monthly for support of institution. . . We believe if this school succeeds with this unique idea of education it's promoters must be southern men who know every phase of Negro life."

Dr. Dillard was impressed with Strange's plea, for the most part because he saw the school as an opportunity to establish a rural Negro public secondary school. A. C. Lewis, Superintendent of Schools for Tangipahoa Parish, was impressed for another reason. He viewed the school as an opportunity to provide training for teachers who would staff the parish's rural black schools.

So the school was established in 1911. Lewis, Strange, and Dillard, along with B. C. Caldwell, Field Agent for the Slater Fund, worked out the details which brought into being the Tangipahoa Parish Training School for Colored Children. The school board furnished teachers and equipment, and the Slater Fund gave assistance in the amount of $500 toward the salary of an industrial teacher for the school. The school was the first "county training school" in the South and one of the first rural public schools providing secondary education for Negroes in the nation. Three other county training schools were established in the South later that same academic year. According to Benjamin Brawley in *Doctor Dillard of the Jeanes Fund* (New York: Fleming H. Revell, 1930, pp. 74–75), four years later there were 42 county training schools, and by 1927 there were 306.

According to A. C. Lewis and W. A. Sisemore, *Special Report on Negro Education in Louisiana: 1923–1924* (Baton Rouge: Louisiana State Department of Education Bulletin N. 104, 1924, pp. 18–21), Tangipahoa Parish Training School in 1923–1924 was one of sixteen parish training schools in the state. Its grounds encompassed 104 acres, and it had eight classrooms and eight teachers. Its enrollment was 205 and average attendance 189. It had 49 high school students, including seven in the eleventh grade (it was the only training school in the state which offered instruction in the eleventh grade). A total of 81 students lived in its two dormitories. It was one of only two training schools in the state which had full 9-month school terms.

The vocational education classes at the school encompassed such subjects as home economics, agriculture, and carpentry. The teacher training course could be undertaken by a student after he or she had completed the eleventh grade. It consisted of an additional year of instruction at the end of which the student would receive a teacher's certificate and academic credit equivalent to one year of college. The teacher training program was usually staffed by professors from the Louisiana Negro Normal School (Grambling College).

The Tangipahoa Parish Training School drew many students from surrounding parishes, including Washington, St. Tammany, St. Helena, East and West Feliciana, and from southern Mississippi, especially Pike County. Thus a dormitory was necessary for the students who could not live at home. School terms usually began in July and ended in March to allow students to participate in the harvesting of the strawberry crop.

The school went through three phases in its development. From its founding in 1911 until 1955 it was known as the Tangipahoa Parish Training School and for most of this period was under the leadership of Oliver Wendell Dillon. From 1955 until 1969, although its operations continued in much the same manner, its name was the O. W. Dillon Memorial School. In 1969 with the coming of integration, it became Kentwood Elementary School.

The Old Dormitory was built in the early 1920s. At first it housed only about fifteen persons, mainly families of the teachers. Later it housed as many as a hundred girls and female teachers. It remained a dormitory until 1951, when it was renovated and converted to classrooms. In recent years it had been used mainly for Home Economics classes and instruction in remedial reading and mathematics.

In recent months plans have been laid for major changes in the school's facilities. The Old Dormitory, one of the two oldest remaining buildings associated with the school, was slated to be demolished. But a movement to save the building has resulted in its removal to another site nearby. Plans are being made for the building to be converted to a combination day-care center for working mothers and museum providing exhibits on the Tangipahoa Parish Training School and black history.

LAFAYETTE (Lafayette Parish)   *421 Carmel Ave., District 7*
Holy Rosary Institute

Holy Rosary Institute was founded in 1913 by the Reverend Philip Keller, a priest of the Diocese of Galveston, Texas, now the Diocese of Galveston/Houston. In its inception, Holy Rosary Institute provided vocational and technical education for black females, thus embodying the racial ideology of Booker T. Washington, who remained the dominant spokesman for blacks in the United States until his death in 1915. The main thrust of Washington's famous 1895 Atlanta speech was that blacks must first establish themselves economically before agitating for social or political equality. He stressed that this economic advancement would come through industrial/technical training. His own Tuskegee in Alabama provided such an education and Holy Rosary Institute reflected Washington's ideas.

In addition, the founding of Holy Rosary must be viewed within its historical context. The late nineteenth and early twentieth century is generally regarded as the nadir of race relations in the United States. Blacks in the South were disfranchised, legally segregated, impoverished, and uneducated. What schools there were for blacks were separate and decidedly inferior. It was within this context that Holy Rosary Institute was founded in 1913.

Holy Rosary also has served as a Normal School to train teachers for rural black schools and is presently one of the few remaining black Catholic high schools in the United States.

From 1913, Holy Rosary Institute has been staffed by the Sisters of the Holy Family, a congregation of black religious women founded in New Orleans in the 1850s. The priests and brothers of the Society of the Divine Word, a religious congregation of men dedicated to the spiritual care of blacks, have been associated with the school since 1930.

LECOMPTE (Rapides Parish) *Off SH 456, near town*
St. John Baptist Church

The St. John Baptist Church is locally significant in the area of architecture because it is an outstanding local example of Eastlake/Queen Anne architecture. It features a variety of elements not found on other buildings of its style in the vicinity. The context for evaluation is the Lecompte/Lamourie area, which is south of Alexandria in Rapides Parish.

St. John Baptist Church is being nominated for significance on the local level because it is the most ornate building of its style in the Lecompte/Lamourie vicinity. Of the approximately 20 Queen Anne buildings that were located during a comprehensive survey of the area, 75% of them were very simple and featured only a few elements that are generally associated with the style. St. John Baptist Church is one of the three most fully developed Queen Anne structures in the area and is further distinguished among these buildings by the following factors:

1. One of the major characteristics of the style is the use of a variety of textures on the surface of the building. With its clapboards, shingles, half-timbering, and panels of "wainscotting," St. John Baptist Church has a wider variety than any of the other buildings of its style in the area;

2. it is the only one with half-timbering;

3. it is the only one with a flared second story;

4. it is the only one with such elaborate Eastlake aprons in the gable peaks;

5. it makes the most profuse use of shingles.

As stated in the description, the exterior of the building is almost completely intact. For buildings of any type of this style, this is becoming increasingly unusual as renovations are made to "economize" on upkeep.

St. John Baptist Church was organized in 1869 as a church for the black residents of Ashton Plantation. The present church building was dedicated on November 11, 1888.

MANSURA (Avoyelles Parish) *SH 107, near town*
St. Paul Lutheran Church

The St. Paul Lutheran Church is of local educational significance because it represents the only educational opportunity available to local black children from its construction in 1916 through the late 1930s, when it ceased to be a school. Full-term classes were held there initially for grades 1–7, with the eighth grade being added in the late 1920s.

The school at St. Paul's must be viewed within its historic context for a full appreciation of its significance. Schools run by religious denominations were among the very few places where blacks could receive a decent education in rural Louisiana from the end of Reconstruction until the post-World War II era. Although there were other educational opportunities available, almost all of them were either of poor quality or of tenuous existence. The home school, where a mother taught groups of neighborhood children, was one alternative. But these only existed sporadically, instruction was not consistent, and the teachers were often poorly educated themselves.

Another alternative was the state-supported school system, such as it was. After Reconstruction, a legislative act provided for a system of separate "public" education for blacks and whites. This was, in effect, more a quasi-public effort because the state provided only a modicum of funding, with local sources providing the building and other necessities. The schools were usually located in churches or lodge buildings, and teachers were poorly qualified. With the retrenchment policies of the day and the general lack of interest in public education, funding was woefully inadequate for even a single-school system, let alone the dual system mandated by segregation. From the beginning, black schools were generally not treated equally in the distribution of funds, and received an increasingly disproportionate share as white schools grew in number and importance. Also, of course, the notion of educating blacks certainly ran contrary to the racial attitudes of the time.

Indeed, black "public schools" were really not schools at all. Essentially meager public subsidies were used to support quasi-private efforts. As T. H. Harris, State Superintendent of Education from 1908–1940, reported in his autobiography: "In most cases Negro churches were used for schoolhouses and the only equipment in these churches were the benches used for church services. The school term was from two to four months and the teachers were uneducated and wholly unequipped to instruct children."

By contrast, a parochial school such as the one at St. Paul Lutheran Church provided a good education with trained, motivated teachers. Indeed, schools run by religious denominations and those supported by private philanthropic funds (such as the Rosenwald schools of the 1920s) were about the only bright spots in black education in rural Louisiana from the end of Reconstruction until the post-World II period.

St. Paul operated as a combination church and school from the very beginning. The present building's predecessor was completed in 1899 with Reverend William Pretzch of Brooklyn as the first pastor and teacher. This building was replaced with the current one in 1916, with classes being held in the wing as well as the church proper. Most of the information about the school comes from interviews with older citizens of Lutherville who were educated there in the 1920s and '30s. Also, there are some records showing the enrollment and subjects taught.

It is clear that Lutherville blacks received a quality education at St. Paul, especially when one considers the alternatives. Initially, grades 1–7 were taught, but the eighth was added in the late 1920s. Teachers were sent by the Lutheran Mission Board and were usually pastor and teacher. Two individuals particularly remembered by former students were Reverend and Mrs. Calvin Peter Thompson, both graduates of a Lutheran "normal school" in New Orleans. School was full-term and lasted all day. Subjects taught were the usual basics such as history, geography, language, and arithmetic. By the 1928–29 term (the last year shown in extant records), there were 72 students. The school served principally the black community of Lutherville (which took its name from the church), but former students indicate that there were also some children from nearby Mansura and Marksville (each about two miles away). Whether there were educational opportunities for blacks in these two communities is unclear, but suffice it to say that St. Paul was certainly the only black school in the immediate Lutherville area. The enrollment figures alone (peaking at about 80) speak to the local educational impact of this small rural school.

MELROSE (Natchitoches Parish)   *SH 119, in town*
Melrose Plantation
Yucca

Melrose Plantation is of great significance both architecturally and historically. Architecturally, its buildings illustrate the changes and variations in local building form and techniques from the earliest French Colonial types to the 1830s period of the Big House, and the late 19th and early 20th century additions. If further research can verify that the design of the African and Ghans houses is indeed African in origin, their significance would be even greater.

The historic significance of Melrose is perhaps more important than its undeniably great architectural worth. Its significance lies in many fields—ethnic, artistic, and literary. The ever-increasing interest in Negro history in the United States adds to the importance of Melrose as a plantation established and developed by free people of color through several generations. This fact lends credance to the assumption that the design of the African House and Ghana House at Melrose are actually African. The Big House is known to have been built in 1833 by Louis Metoyer, Jr., a free man of color.

Melrose is also important as the house of Mrs. Cammie Garrett Henry, whose patronage of the arts and preservation of local artifacts was the beginning of a movement to preserve the heritage of Natchitoches Parish. Her enthusiasm for the state's history and folkways inspired others to seek out, to preserve, and to protect reminders of the past. Her house was a mecca for authors, artists, architects, horticulturists, and those interested in the various handcrafts that she revived.

Among writers who resided at Melrose was Lyle Saxon who lived in Yucca House and worked on some of his books there, making use of Mrs. Henry's vast collection of scrapbooks. The French journalist Francois Mignon lived at Melrose until 1970 and produced a series of decorative plates illustrating the historic Natchitoches area, tape recordings of a visit to Melrose and some writing. The noted Negro primitive artist Clementine Hunter painted a panorama of Louisiana plantation life on the walls of the upper room of the African House.

MONROE (Ouachita Parish)   *916 Adams St., in town*
St. James United Methodist Church

St. James United Methodist Church is locally significant in the area of architecture as a rare example of the Gothic Revival style within the context of Monroe.

The comprehensive structures survey has identified over 1,350 structures in the city that are 50 years old or older. The vast majority of these are relatively plain shotgun houses, cottages, and bungalows. Monroe also contains some impressive residences (mainly in some form of the classical style), along with a downtown commercial district (NR) which features mainly neo-classical and Italianate buildings. St. James Church is significant as one of only two convincing examples of the Gothic Revival style in Monroe. The only other hint of the historic Gothic Revival taste one can find in the city is in a few bungalows which feature a shallow pointed arch here or there.

NEW ORLEANS (Orleans Parish)   *Rampart at St. Peter,*
in the French Quarter

Congo Square

Congo Square is locally significant in the area of ethnic heritage because it was the focus of an important aspect of New Orleans' African-American history. Beginning in the early nineteenth century and continuing up to roughly the Civil War, the square was the site of slave dances on Sundays. In the early days, the dances and music were African, but by the 1830s and '40s, American Culture had made its impact.

It should be noted that African-Americans were a very important group in the history and development of antebellum New Orleans. While there are a great many historic properties associated with them, either as slaves or free people of color, Congo Square is believed to be the only site which is specifically and compellingly associated with the retention of their African heritage. It was also a major focal point of that heritage, being a place where at times hundreds congregated. According to historian Gary A. Donaldson, "Congo Square was the focal point of a subculture of New Orleans black slaves who carried on a lifestyle as close as possible to what they had remembered from their earlier lives in Africa (or what they had been told Africa was like)." He concludes: "The importance of Congo Square cannot be underestimated as an attempt by African slaves to hold on to what they could of their heritage."

The most well-known account of the legendary dances at Congo Square was left us by Benjamin Latrobe, who happened to stumble upon the square one Sunday afternoon in 1819. He was walking up St. Peter Street and heard "a most extraordinary noise," which he thought must have come from "some horse mill, the horses trampling on a wooden floor." He found, however, that it came from a "crowd of 5 or 600 persons assembled in an open space or public square." Blacks "were formed into circular groups in the midst of which was a ring . . . ten feet in diameter." He observed in one ring two women dancing: "They held each a coarse handkerchief, extended by the corners, in their hands . . ." "The music," Latrobe continued, "consisted of two drums and a stringed instrument." He described an old man who played a large cylindrical drum, beating it "with incredible quickness with the edge of his hand and fingers." Together with a second smaller drum, "they made an incredible noise." Latrobe described the stringed instrument as a "most curious instrument . . . which no doubt was imported from Africa." The carving on top of the finger board was "the rude figure of a man in a sitting posture." "The body," he added, "was a calabash. It was played upon by a very little old man, apparently eighty or ninety years old."

Latrobe described another instrument that "consisted of a block cut into something of the form of a cricket bat, with a long and deep mortise down the center. . . ." He also observed an instrument in the shape of "a calabash with a round hold in it, the hold studded with brass nails. . . ." It was beaten by a woman with two short sticks. "A man sung an uncouth song to the dancing which I suppose was in some African language, for it was not French," wrote Latrobe. He concluded that "the amusements of Sunday, have, it seems, perpetuated here, those of Africa among its inhabitants." The description was accompanied by sketches of some of the instruments.

Latrobe's account is of the square in the heyday of its African heritage. Scholars have noted the strong similarities between the instruments used and native African instruments, and the circles in the dances are believed to represent different tribes. By the 1830s, American influence had begun to make itself felt, and as time went on, the activities became less and less specifically African. However, as late as 1845, a reporter witnessed in the square what he called "regular Ethiopian breakdowns." He noted that the happy crowd was equipped with "rude instruments of their own contrivance, the like of which we have never seen before." The last known period account (A. Oakey Hall, *The Manhattener in New Orleans,* 1851) spoke of "clattering bones, and barrelheaded drumming."

NEW ORLEANS (Orleans Parish)   *District 2, between St. Claude Ave.*
and the Mississippi River,
Esplanade Ave. and Press St.

Faubourg Marigny Historic District

The significance of the Faubourg Marigny area is found in the architectural integrity of its many streets of Creole, Greek Revival, and Victorian cottages; its mansions, townhouses, churches, warehouses, and corner residential-commercial structures. Of equal importance is the area's heritage.

Pierre Philippe Marigny was among the richest men in the New World. His vast land holdings in Louisiana centered around New Orleans, with property both across Lake Ponchartrain (in what has become Mandeville) and immediately downriver from the Vieux Carre. The Marigny Plantation house, located near New Orleans and described as twice the size of normal plantations, was where Pierre entertained the Duc d'Orleans (later King Louis Philippe) and his two brothers in 1798. Among the favors bestowed upon the visitors was a generous loan, which was apparently never repaid.

In 1800 Pierre died, and 15-year-old Bernard Xavier Phillippe de Marigny de Mandeville, the third child and oldest son, was sent to Pensacola by his guardian, de Lino de Chalmette. Bernard did not seem to be interested in absorbing the business education he was supposed to receive there, and so he was sent to London with the hopes that he would do better in England. However, he spent much time in Paris and ran up very large bills, so, in 1803 he returned to Louisiana.

In 1804 he married Mary Ann Jones, the daughter of the former American consul in New Orleans. This marriage was very successful and prompted Bernard Marigny to begin his long career as a politician and statesman for the City of New Orleans and later for the State of Louisiana. Unfortunately, in 1808 his first wife died and shortly thereafter he married Ann Mathilda Morales, daughter of Don Ventura Morales, former Spanish Intendant and Royal Contador. The second marriage was not a happy one and his earlier profligate habits continued, and he began selling property, probably to pay his gambling debts.

In 1805 Marigny applied to the New Orleans City Council for permission to subdivide his property just downriver from the Vieux Carre. The plans were drawn by Nicholas de Finiels and the streets were laid out by Barthelemy Lafon (both prominent architects, engineers, and surveyors of the time). Land was sold into the 1820s.

The Faubourg Marigny eventually became the Third Municipality of New Orleans under a system that divided the city into three districts.

Marigny meanwhile became very interested in politics, and was elected to the state Legislature in 1810, to the Constitutional Convention in 1812, to the House and Senate for several years, and finally to the Constitutional Convention in 1845.

He gradually lost his property and wealth, although he is still considered the model of the affluent, influential Creole gentleman. He died in 1868 after a fall.

The subdivision grew rapidly and the architecture reflects the diverse economic and cultural involvements of the area. The early Creole cottages that surrounded the Marigny Plantation House were often small truck farms that supplied the French Market and the corner stores of the area.

The vertical and horizontal mixture of land use added to the character and vitality of the area. The corner store usually had the proprietor's residence above or apartments there, and this pattern was maintained in the many commercial establishments of Frenchmen Street, which was second only to Canal Street for shopping in both the 19th and 20th century.

The industrial activity of Faubourg Marigny began with the Marigny Canal and the sawmill near the edge of the Mississippi River. Bernard Marigny renamed this section the Champ Elysees, now known as Elysian Fields Avenue and still the major circulation avenue of the area. Subsequently, industry expanded along the river with the construction of warehouses.

The landscape architecture of Marigny is significant in its lively and human-scaled streetscapes focused on Washington Square, originally called Place Washington and given to the people of the "Place" by Marigny. It is the only square in New Orleans planted with a double alley of live oaks. Around this square were built some of the grandest mansions of the area.

Early Creoles and their descendants, many of aristocratic background, prided themselves on their lineage. Later, when light persons of color, descendants of freedmen who also nurtured a pride of race, referred to themselves as "Creoles", and when non-Southern Americans naively accepted the term to imply ethnic mixture, those Creoles who considered themselves pure-blooded resented this interpretation. The Marigny area, however, is distinctive for its proud light-colored families, for its large German population that became assimilated into a predominately Latin attitude and lifestyle, as well as a large influx of Filipinos, Italians, and others. The particular character of the neighborhood is derived from this very tradition of mixture, which has defied definition. The term "Creole" is therefore appropriate in relation to Marigny, its architecture, folkways, lifestyle, and its relaxed and tolerant attitude—by the very fact that the term itself has taken on an increasing elusiveness, while at the same time has acquired a particular validity for this area, however irregular as to any kind of precisely definable limits.

Typically Marigny residents are from families that have lived in Marigny for several generations or new, young residents who have been attracted to this area by the spirit of revitalization found here. Older houses are being renovated and restored.

NEW ORLEANS (Orleans Parish)   *Louisiana Ave. and LaSalle St.*
Flint-Goodridge Hospital of Dillard University

Flint-Goodridge Hospital is of state and local significance in the area of health/medicine because of the roles it played in providing professional training for black physicians in Louisiana and health care for the black citizens of New Orleans.

The ascent of blacks from the status of second-class citizens to full enjoyment of the benefits and opportunites of American life has many aspects to it, ranging from voting rights to education. A significant but often overlooked aspect is medicine, both treatment of the sick and the training of physicians. While the white population benefited from the medical advances of the late nineteenth and early twentieth centuries, to a large extent the black population did not. For example, a 1930 report showed the death rate among blacks in New Orleans to be twice that of whites. Another example was infant mortality. a staggering 12% among the city's blacks. The 1930 report also pointed to the problem of training black physicians: "While there are, for instance, about 140 colored graduates annually from the medical schools of both the South and the North, there are only 40 internships available to them throughout the country. . ."

The Flint-Goodridge Hospital was actually founded in 1911, and the present building represents an overall effort to expand and improve its operations. It was conceived and built as the medical unit of the newly created Dillard University. During the 1930s, Flint-Goodridge was the only institution in Louisiana offering medical internships for blacks. The staff consisted of nineteen white doctors (mostly teachers) and twenty-nine active staff doctors (all black). It was also the only place in the state where black nurses could receive professional training. From the first, the 88-bed hospital was fully accredited. Except for Charity Hospital, which was for indigents, Flint-

Goodridge was the only hospital in New Orleans that admitted blacks. A 1938 article in the *Times-Picayune* praising the hospital pointed particularly to contributions in the area of tuberculosis testing and treatment, infant and maternal care, and the treatment of syphilis.

NEW ORLEANS (Orleans Parish)   *571 Audubon Street*
James H. Dillard House

James Hardy Dillard was born October 24, 1856, at the family plantation in the tidewater region of Virginia. His family were landed aristrocracy in the Southern tradition. Farmer's Delight, as the plantation was called, consisted of extensive land and 350 slaves. The Civil War ended the family's affluence, but it did not change his parents' attitudes on a correct, traditional education for their son.

Dillard received his early education from his mother and from a neighboring teacher who held classes in a nearby Baptist Church. At the age of twelve he was sent to live with his aunt in Norfolk, Virginia. There he attended a private school conducted by a William R. Galt. Galt's school stressed the traditional curriculum with its emphasis on language, mathematics, and history. Here Dillard completed his secondary education.

In 1873 he entered Washington and Lee, where he graduated in 1875 with high honors. In 1876 he completed his Master of Arts degree and a year later won the additional degree of Bachelor of Laws. Although Dillard had wanted to practice law, he turned instead to the teaching profession.

His first position was the principalship of the Rodman School at Norfolk. In 1882 he was appointed co-principal of the Norfolk Academy, a position he held for the next five years. During his ten years as a secondary school administrator and instructor, Dillard published a number of articles on pedagogical subjects and a mathematics textbook. For several years he also taught at the Sauveur Summer School of languages at several northern colleges. Thanks to his publication record and his work at the college level, Dillard was appointed in 1887 to the principalship of the Women's College of Washington University in St. Louis. He remained in St. Louis until 1891, when Col. William P. Johnson, an old friend and teacher, called him to Tulane University in New Orleans as a professor of Latin.

Dillard was thirty-five when he moved to New Orleans and entered on his new duties. Up until that time his experience had been closely tied to the life of a school administrator and teacher. By 1894 he had been elected Dean of Tulane's College of Arts and Sciences. He was also very active in civic affairs, becoming president of the public library and president of the Child Welfare Association. At one time his fellow citizens urged him to run for mayor. As a university dean and civic leader, Dillard seemed well on the way to becoming an established and respected member of New Orleans society. Although as an educator Dillard had always been aware of the problems of black education, his experience in New Orleans brought a fundamental change in his position. The decade of the 1890s was a particularly brutal period in white-black relations. White supremacy was the rule of the day and lynchings an all too frequent occurrence. These outrages deeply offended Dillard's aristocratic sense of justice and civilization and stimulated him to a deeper examination of the "Negro problem."

Dillard approached the "Negro problem" from the perspective of the educator. His first step was to violate local taboos when he publically shook hands and conversed with white instructors who taught in the black colleges in the area. Up to this time, these teachers had been ostracized by better New Orleans society. As president of the public library, he used his influence to promote the construction of a Carnegie library for black citizens. He widened his contacts with his fellow educators in the black schools and by 1905 he was a trustee of the major black colleges in the New Orleans vicinity, Straight and New Orleans University.

In 1907 the trustees of the newly constituted Jeanes Fund offered Dillard the directorship of the fund. The Jeanes Fund, which was established in the will of Miss Anna T. Jeanes, a wealthy Philadelphia Quaker, was dedicated to helping the black rural schools in the South. At first Dillard did not want the position. His colleagues urged him to accept the offer, pointing out that he was one of only a few men who had gained respect and prestige in both white and black educational circles. Dillard changed his mind. In 1908 he resigned from Tulane and entered on his new duties.

Dr. Dillard directed the Negro Rural School Fund from 1908 to 1931. In 1917 he also became president of the Slater Fund, another philanthropic foundation which supported county training institutes for black teachers. Dillard merged the administration of the two funds.

When he retired in 1931, he had made a major impact on education in the South. In addition to his work for the Jeanes and Slater Funds, Dillard was a member of the General Education Board and the Southern Education Board, an official of the Phelps-Stokes Fund, a member of the Board of Visitors of the College of William and Mary, and a founder of Bettis Academy at Trenton, South Carolina. He received many honors, among them honorary doctor of law degrees from Sewanee and Harvard. When in 1929 Straight and

New Orleans University merged, the new school was named Dillard University in his honor.

After retirement, Dillard moved to Charlottesville, Virginia. In retirement, he continued his interest in black education. He conducted an extensive correspondence and his council was continuously sought. On August 2, 1940, he died quietly in his sleep.

James H. Dillard's significance in the history of black education is derived from his directorship of the Jeanes and Slater Funds. With men like Atticus G. Haygood of Atlanta and J. L. M. Curry of Alabama, Dillard gave shape and direction to the philanthropic programs that were an indispensible financial support to black education. Two major programs are especially associated with Dillard. The first was the Jeanes teachers. When in 1907 Jackson Davis suggested to Dillard that Miss Virginia Randolph of Richmond, Virginia, be employed to introduce her vocational teaching methods throughout Henrico county, Dillard embraced the program. The Jeanes Negro Rural School Fund paid Miss Randolph's salary. As the Jeanes supervisor program became a success, the Jeanes Fund spread the idea throughout the South, spending the bulk of its monies paying the salaries of Jeanes supervisors.

The second program associated with Dillard, this time in his capacity as director of the Slater Fund, was the county training institute. Dillard is said to have conceived and instituted this program himself. Under the program, black teachers in the public schools met yearly on a county-wide basis to attend teacher training courses. The Slater Fund provided the funds for the institutes. Both the Jeanes supervisor and the county training institute programs expanded black elementary and secondary education and improved its quality. A major result was that the black colleges gradually dropped their elementary and secondary education programs. They thus could concentrate their energies and resources on providing an emerging black leadership with a higher quality education.

In addition to the Jeanes and Slater Funds' programs, Dillard also influenced other programs. Through his membership on Rockefeller's General Education Board, the Southern Education Board, and the Phelps-Stokes Fund, he made inputs to the black education programs of these important organizations.

Dillard's role in black education was a reflection of the contradictions inherent in black education in the South at the beginning of the twentieth century. He accepted the basic premises of Southern society. The South dictated a biracial arrangement of its people. As Henry Allen Bullock writes, "Negroes were to be kept socially isolated from whites by means of a rigid system of residential segregation; they were to be limited to special occupational pursuits by means of job restrictions; they were to be tailored to 'Negro ways' through a rigid code of interracial etiquette; and they were to be reinforced in their obedience to caste rules through formal schooling." For the Negro, formal schooling meant primarily a "special education" that corresponded to his position in Southern society. That special education was to be generally vocational in nature, and it was vocational education that Dillard supported and promoted in his public statements and through his direction of such programs as the Jeanes teacher and the county training institutes. In a letter of instruction to all teachers in the Jeanes supervisor program, he wrote, "You should introduce into the schools such simple forms of industrial work as may be needful and helpful, and will tend to show the connection between the school and the daily life of the community." Dillard participated in maintaining the traditional "Southern way of life."

At the same time, his sixty-year dedication and devotion to the cause of black education reflected his personal commitment to improving the well-being of black Americans. The activities of the Jeanes and Slater Funds were directed to promoting self-help for all blacks who had thrown down their buckets where they were. In stimulating white and black support for Negro education, these programs and others like them did in fact give blacks the opportunity, first, to improve their social and economic condition and second, and more importantly, to cultivate slowly an educated black leadership which would later challenge the fundamental assumptions of a society which had created Negro education as a separate concern within American education. Dillard worked with the social realities as he found them. His admirers claim that his was a position of pragmatic realism.

An assessment of the significance of James Hardy Dillard in the history of American education is open to all the contradictions inherent in interpreting the history of black-white relations in America. It is, however, a fact that he, and the deeds of philanthropy he symbolizes, played an important role in the history of black education during the first decades of this century.

NEW ORLEANS (Orleans Parish)   *222 North Roman St.*
St. James A.M.E. Church

The St. James A.M.E. Church is architecturally significant on the state level because it is an unusually opulent and "high style" example of an A.M.E. church within the context of Louisiana. Most A.M.E. churches in the state were humble, unpretentious structures. By contrast, St. James is a relatively highly ornamented statement in the Victorian Gothic Revival style. It is probably the most pretentious A.M.E. church building in Louisiana.

Significant Gothic-style features of the church (after the 1903 renovation) include:

1. the pointed arch fenestration;
2. the stained glass windows;
3. the blind arcading;
4. the corner pinnacles; and
5. the central open spire.

The first two features are sometimes found on late nineteenth and early twentieth century A.M.E. churches in Louisiana, but the last three are almost unknown.

The St. James A.M.E. Church traces its origins to 1844, when a group of free men of color organized themselves into a religious society under the name of the African Methodist Episcopal Church of New Orleans. The formation of this group was the result of the mistreatment of its members by the Wesley Chapel M.E. Church, a white congregation which accepted free people of color as members. The new congregation was headed by Thomas Doughty. The growth of the church membership necessitated the construction of a permanent church building, and the lots on which St. James presently stands were purchased in 1848 and construction was completed by 1851. At that time Doughty was sent to the Indiana Conference of the African Methodist Episcopal Church for the purpose of bringing the church into the conference. He was cordially received and was appointed the first pastor of St. James A.M.E. Church. The church retained its original half-Greek, half-Gothic appearance until 1903, when it was heavily Gothicized in the late Victorian manner.

NEW ORLEANS (Orleans Parish)   *1201 Cadiz St., District 2*
St. Peter African Methodist Episcopal Church

St. Peter African Methodist Episcopal Church is significant in the areas of black history, "social/humanitarian," and architecture. As a congregation, St. Peter African Methodist Episcopal Church dates from about 1850 and is the oldest black congregation in the former community of Jefferson City and one of the oldest in the New Orleans area. In addition, the church has played an extensive role in the life of the surrounding community, and architecturally, the present church building is one of the most outstanding black churches in the state.

Although St. Peter's African Methodist Episcopal Church has been modified over the years, it retains a degree of architectural significance owing to its size and to its use of two high-style features which are seldom found in black churches. These are the shingle-style side tower and the relatively elaborate stained-glass windows of the nave.

The building seems to have been constructed in 1858 as the (white) Jefferson City Methodist Episcopal Church South. St. Peter African Methodist Episcopal Church was associated with the building almost from the first as the white church permitted the blacks to worship on the ground floor of the building while the white congregation worshipped upstairs. The St. Peter African Methodist Episcopal Church had begun in 1850, when a group of black people started worshipping together in a small house at Prytania and Valmont streets near the location of the building. They were followers of the principles of Richard Allen (1760–1831), who had founded the African Methodist Episcopal Church in 1787 in Philadelphia, Pennsylvania.

During the same year as its construction (1858), the building was damaged by a storm, and the black people helped the whites repair it. But this harmonious relationship between the two groups did not last, because tension between them arose as the Civil War approached, and soon the blacks were no longer allowed to worship on the ground floor. In the early 1860s, the black congregation assembled at a house at Plaquemine (later Coliseum) and Bordeaux streets, a few blocks from the church building.

Late in the 1860s, St. Peter African Methodist Episcopal Church was incorporated in Jefferson City under the state Statute of Corporations of 1849. In 1867, the congregation purchased and moved into a building on two lots of the square bounded by Coliseum, Chestnut, Bordeaux, and Valance streets. The membership increased steadily over the next few years, and a larger building was soon needed.

Meanwhile, the membership of the (white) Jefferson City Methodist Episcopal Church South had grown, and in 1876 it moved to a new building at 3900 St. Charles Avenue. It is now known as the Rayne Memorial United Methodist Church. On March 31, 1877, the white congregation sold their old building to the St. Peter African Methodist Episcopal Church in return for a consideration of $4,000. This was, of course, the same building on whose ground floor the African Methodist Episcopal Church had worshipped prior to the Civil War.

John Blassingame's *Black New Orleans: 1860–1880* (Chicago, 1973) provides a means of placing St. Peter's African Methodist Episcopal Church in some degree of perspective with other black churches in the New Orleans area in that period. Blassingame notes that during 1860–1880, "the strongest Protestant church in the Negro community was the African Methodist Epsicopal." In 1860, he notes, there were four African Methodist Episcopal churches in New Orleans. (This figure probably does include St. Peter, since Jefferson City was annexed in 1870.)

The church building has been twice remodeled since 1877, once in 1890 and again in 1924. The only names of the building's architects and contractors available are for 1924. The architect was Edward Ganet, and the contractor was A.L. Riley. The cost of the remodeling work of 1924 was $6,000.

There are no figures available on the church's membership prior to 1915, as extensive church records do not survive from that time. Between 1915 and 1960, the membership totaled over 400. The current membership is about 300.

St. Peter African Methodist Episcopal Church has always played an important role in the life of the neighborhood around it, particularly in the twentieth century. In the 1920s, the church provided space in its ground floor for practical nursing classes taught by the staff of Touro Infirmary. During the 1930s, it provided similar space for secretarial and business classes. It also provided space for an employment office associated with the relief programs of the New Deal, especially the WPA. People would come into the office and register for work. They were put to work on various government projects in return for food, clothing, and a small cash income.

During the 1950s, the church again provided space for practical nursing classes, this time taught by staff from the public schools. In 1954, local chapters of the Boy Scouts of America and the Explorers were organized at the church. In 1956, a chapter of the Cub Scouts was organized. In 1974, the Cub Scout pack was awarded a citation by President Nixon.

During the Civil Rights Movement of the 1960s, the church provided space on its ground floor for classes in voter registration taught by students from Tulane and Loyola universities.

St. Peter African Methodist Episcopal Church is also the mother church for three other African Methodist Episcopal churches in the area: Mount Zion African Methodist Episcopal Church in Bridge City, which dates from the early 1950s; St. Peter African Methodist Epsicopal Church in Carrollton, which dates from 1920; and St. Luke African Methodist Episcopal Church, located at the corner of Congress and Florida Walk streets, which dates from 1924.

Prominent citizens who have been members of St. Peter African Methodist Episcopal Church include Israel M. Augustine, Jr., Judge, Section I, Criminal District Court, Parish of Orleans; Duplain Rhodes, Jr., prominent businessman; and Dr. William R. Adams, Jr., surgeon.

OSCAR (Pointe Coupee Parish)   *One-half mile from intersection of SH 1 and Major Lane, near town*

Cherie Quarters Cabins

The two Cherie Quarters Cabins are of state significance in the area of architecture because they are rare surviving examples of a once common antebellum building type which has all but disappeared from the state.

The census schedules of 1860 reveal that there were approximately 1,640 holdings of 50 or more slaves in Louisiana on the eve of the Civil War. In addition, there were innumerable holdings of less than 50. This information, along with various other sources, indicates that at one time there must easily have been thousands of slave cabins across the state. They were a very predominant feature of the rural landscape, vastly outnumbering the plantation houses. However, today this situation is reversed. A number of antebellum plantation houses have survived, but it is highly unusual for a plantation to retain any slave dwellings. Although no comprehensive survey of slave quarters has been undertaken in Louisiana, staff knowledge concerning their numbers and locations indicates that only about 40–50 survive. As extremely rare examples of a once common antebellum building type, the Cherie Quarters Cabins are strong candidates for National Register listing.

The River Lake workers' cabins have been known as Cherie Quarters since some time after 1892, when Pervis Cherie Major purchased River Lake from the Arthur Denis estate. A member of an old False River family, Major hired a teacher for the black children who lived on his new property. Eventually, the workers' quarters acquired his name.

Cherie Quarters is the birthplace of Ernest J. Gaines, prominent African-American author of such noted works as *The Autobiography of Miss Jane Pittman* (1971), *A Gathering of Old Men* (1983), and *A Lesson Before Dying* (1994). Although the cabin in which Gaines was born in 1933 is no longer standing, the community which centered upon the quarters row exercised a major influence upon his writing.

The two Cherie Quarters cabins are also of state significance under Criterion A in the area of ethnic history because of their direct association with slave labor which, of course, was crucial to the state's plantation economy during the antebellum period. Plantations, which were originally developed in eighth-century India, represent a distinctive form of agricultural practice which came to predominate in the states of the old Confederacy. Plantation regions, both in Africa and in the new world, relied upon several factors: (1) land available in large units, generally several hundred acres at least; (2) a marketable cash crop; (3) easy bulk processing techniques; (4) cheap transportation to bring the cash crop to national and even international markets; and importantly, (5) an abundant supply of landless rural labor to work the crop.

According to cultural geographer Dr. Milton Newton: "Only slavery could fulfill the labor profile wanted by the planter. Indians failed as slaves because of disease, refusal to be enslaved, and the ease of escaping to a sympathetic group. Whites failed as slaves for the same reasons. (Blacks) succeeded as slaves because of their color, which made it easy to police for runaways and because of the horrible stringent 'selection' that capture and shipment levied upon their number. Weak, sickly, and truculent individuals were eliminated in the slave pens of Africa, in the slave ships, and (in the) slave markets."

By their very nature, dwellings such as those at Cherie Quarters provide us a glimpse into what one historian has termed "the world the slaves made." And it is a rare glimpse, given the relative paucity of surviving resources of this type. One might note that surviving examples as well as a few other sources such as accounts from the period reveal that the cabins at Cherie Quarters appear to be typical for antebellum Louisiana.

PORT HUDSON (East Baton Rouge Parish) *In town*
Port Hudson Battlefield & McCallum House

Two regiments of the Louisiana Native Guards of Free Colored, the 1st and the 3rd, participated in a Union assault on Port Hudson, a Confederate stronghold on the lower Mississippi, in 1863. These black troops had evoked considerable discussion and speculation in the North, in Banks' Military Department, in Washington, and throughout military circles as to their value as fighting troops. The question, "Will the Negro fight?" had yet to be answered so far as many onlookers were concerned. The black troops were aware of this challenge and welcomed the decision to use them in a severe test where they could demonstrate their fighting ability.

The 1st Regiment of the Louisiana Native Guards was comprised of free black men who were the elite black population of New Orleans and nearby areas. They had an average net worth of $25,000 per man. Many of them were well above the average in intelligence and followed skilled occupations. The outfit had been authorized and its officers commissioned by Confederate Governor Moore of Louisiana in 1861. When New Orleans capitulated to the Federal Government, 26 April 1863, the organization offered its services to General Benjamin Butler who recognized it, commissioned its officers, and encouraged the organization of other similar units into what was called the Corps d'Afrique. All of the line officers of the organization were black men of substance and influence in the community, many of literary and educational achievement.

One of the most popular and efficient officers of this regiment was Captain Andre Cailloux, a black man. A splendid horseman, excellent sportsman, finely educated in Paris and highly polished, he was a leader of the highest quality. Cailloux, a well-to-do man who could certainly have avoided the risks of battle had he chosen to, encouraged his troops for the final attack despite a shattered arm. He died running ahead of them, crying, "Follow me," in French and then in English. Cailloux was honored with a public funeral on 11 July 1863. After a eulogy at St. Rose of Lima Church in New Orleans, a lengthy procession of some thirty-seven black societies and the band of the Forty-Seventh Massachusetts Regiment, Cailloux's remains were interred with military honors in the Bienville Cemetery. In New Orleans, the American flag remained at half mast in his honor for thirty days.

Sergeant Planciancois was at Port Hudson with the 1st Regiment, too. When given the charge to defend the colors, Planciancois replied, "Colonel, I will bring back these colors to you in honor, or report to God the reason why."

The 3rd Regiment consisted mainly of ex-slaves enrolled and organized in New Orleans, 24 November 1862. The black officers who had been largely reponsible for raising the troops were forced to resign when they entered Union service in the Corps d'Afrique and were replaced with white officers.

The third black organization at Port Hudson was the 1st Regiment of Engineers of the Corps d'Afrique. This unit was organized on 28 April 1863 at Camp Parapet, Carrollton, Louisiana. On 24 May, upon order of Major Houston, Chief Engineer, Department of the Gulf, it proceeded to Port Hudson, General Bank's Headquarters, where it arrived on the 26th of May. The following day it received orders from Banks to report to General Weitzel, commanding the right wing.

The 1st and 3rd Regiments of black troops, having received orders the night preceding, that they would attack the enemy on the extreme right of the national line, assumed battle stance early on the morning of 27 May 1863. Numbering 1,080 men, they formed into four lines, the first two were led by Lieutenant-Colonel Bassett and the second two by Lieutenant-Colonel Finnegas with Colonel Nelson placed in command as Brigadier-General.

After artillery preparation and while the guns fired, Banks planned to attack the enemy simultaneously with his whole line. But plans miscarried, timing and communications were off, and the assault became piecemeal with severe fighting developing on the right, especially the extreme right where the black columns were posted.

The black men moved forward in quick time, soon followed by double time. The alignment was perfect and the movement was executed smartly as they entered the woods immediately in front of them. Emerging from the obstacle-ridden woods, they continued their charge towards the works in full face of the batteries. The first fire of the enemy, grape, canister, shell, and musketry, which increased in momentum and concentration as the blacks advanced, killed and wounded a number of them. Wavering momentarily, the blacks, encouraged by Colonel Bassett and the black officers who moved among the men urging them forward with their fearless examples, closed ranks and continued the charge. Every advancing step took its toll in casualties, yet the blacks fought and bled their way through the sheets of fire until they were within fifty paces of the enemy line when they were halted by an unexpected impassable stream, eight feet deep and twenty to forty feet wide, made by the backflow of the river.

Suffering severe losses and stopped by the stream, the troops retired under a continuous fire, regrouped, and charged again, reaching the ditch some fifty feet from the enemy guns. Again they met sheets of enemy fire. In spite of this, a number of volunteers from the decimated Companies E and G, 3rd Native Guards, attempted with their officers to swim across the flooded ditch while covered by the fire of Bassett and Finnegas which temporarily drove the enemy from their outer works. Although some reached the other side and momentarily faced the enemy, it was largely in vain as the water was too much. Only six returned from the party of thirty-five or forty that succeeded in crossing.

Repulsed by the second assault, Nelson sent word to Brigadier General Dwight at the northwestern end of Port Hudson acquainting him with the situation and the insurmountable difficulty, and awaited further orders. They were told to carry on. For the third time the troops dressed into line for assault and charged. Their charge again was met by a holocaust of fire. Yet with a final desperate spurt they pushed on again to within fifty yards of the Rebel battery. So strong was this final charge that a newspaper reporter observing the battle wrote, "Indeed, if only ordinarily supported by artillery and reserves, no one can convince us that they would not have opened a passage through the enemy's works."

Although this statement is speculative, there is no doubt that Banks' attack suffered from being uncoordinated. On the right, next to the black troops, Generals Weitzel, Grover, and Payne made a vigorous atack. General Augur in the center did not mount his attack until long past noon, and Sherman on the left, not until later in the day. This situation enabled the enemy to concentrate its fire on each assaulting group separately with devastating results, especially on the black troops. The blacks remained in action before the enemy line until 4:00 p.m. that afternoon when the order for retreat came. They responded by marching off proudly as if on parade. Port Hudson was not taken, but black soldiers had given a fine account of themselves. Their casualty list easily confirmed this—37 killed, 155 wounded, and 116 missing. Here, as elsewhere on the battlefield, they demonstrated their courage and ability as fighting men.

The role of the black soldiers at Port Hudson is of national historical importance because blacks fought valiantly under black leadership despite extremely heavy losses from their ranks, including the loss of their very popular leader, Captain Callioux; and because free blacks who could have isolated themselves from the struggle of their slave brothers chose instead to sacrifice the security and comfort of their position to fight for the freedom of their people.

The McCallum House (c. 1845) is located on a gravel road near the center of the old Port Hudson tract. It is a simple frame galleried cottage with two front doors, two front windows, a pitched roof, a chimney at each end, and two principal rooms. It appears from "ghost marks" that at one time the house had a pair of rear cabinets with a long central room between, but these rooms have been incorporated into the rest of the house. Today the floor plan consists of a central dividing wall with a single large room on one side and a smaller room on the other with an even smaller room behind it. There is also a rear wing which was apparently built as a separate structure in about 1870 and appended to the house in about 1900.

For a cottage, the house has exceptionally fine detailing such as beaded clapboards on the front and bolection moldings around the windows and in the door panels. Each of the two fireplaces has a mantel, and although they have very typical 1840s moldings, both appear to have been extensively repaired, if not rebuilt.

"Ghost marks" indicate that originally the house had five columns; today it has four. In addition, the clapboarding on the side elevations has been replaced in kind, and one of the chimneys has been lost.

Despite all the changes the McCallum House has undergone, it still should be noted as a contributing element in the Port Hudson Battlefield listing. It has its original massing, fenestration, and most of its exterior detailing. Moreover, the floor plan, with two large front rooms, is similar to the original. After the siege of Port Hudson, this galleried cottage, known as the McCallum House, was one of only three structures standing in an otherwise decimated townscape. There is no doubt that someone surveying that scene would recognize the house today in its open, rather rural, setting. In addition, there are only two structures remaining in the general battlefield area which actually date from the time of the battle. Of these, the McCallum House is by far the better preserved. The other house was completely renovated in the Queen Anne style, complete with new massing, a new porch, and a second story.

The McCallum House's link with the Battle of Port Hudson is both direct and compelling. When the siege began, the house, along with the rest of the town of Port Hudson, was evacuated by the civilian population and turned over to Confederate troops for their use. After the siege, the McCallum House was one of three structures left standing in the town. These were all turned over to Union troops for their use. Today the McCallum House is the only one of these three to survive. (The previously mentioned house which was renovated in the Queen Ann style is some distance from the town site and, for the record, it is not within the battlefield listing boundaries.)

RAYVILLE (Richland Parish) *SH 135, near town*
Poplar Chapel A.M.E. Church

Poplar Chapel is of local architectural significance as a rare and early example of a vernacular rural black church within the context of northeast Louisiana.

Poplar Chapel is fairly typical of churches associated with rural black congregations from across the South during the late nineteenth and early twentieth centuries. It has the basic basilican form with square head windows and an elementary chancel. As with many of the finer examples, the principal elevation is accented with a pair of square towers culminating in pyramidal steeples. These are remotely related to the late nineteenth-century Romanesque Revival. Poplar Chapel also features a modicum of Queen Anne treatment in its imbricated shingled band across the front.

Churches of this ilk were undoubtedly the grandest architectural manifestations of rural black life and culture during the period. Expressing the highest aspirations of each community, they were far more pretentious than sharecropper cabins, cotton houses, and plantation stores. This pretention can be seen at Poplar Chapel in its relatively monumental facade with its twin pyramidal towers and its imbricated shingle ornamentation. Churches like Poplar Chapel have not survived in great numbers in northeastern

Louisiana. Many were abandoned by rural black populations as they immigrated to the cities. Others, where the congregation survived, were either replaced or were bricked over to give them a new look. As far as the State Historic Preservation Office is aware, Poplar Chapel is one of only two pre-World War I rural black churches that survive in the region with any degree of integrity.

RESERVE (St. John the Baptist Parish)   *1628 SH 44, in town*
Godchaux-Reserve Plantation House

Reserve Plantation House is of state significance as an unusually large and important example of the French Creole architectural tradition.

The principal story of any Creole house, the *premier etage,* was from the owner's standpoint the most important place. It was here that the family lived. It was also the focus of whatever architectural refinement the house may have had. Among the few hundred Creole residences that remain in the state, Reserve is conspicuous because of the size of its premier etage. As far as the State Historic Preservation Office is aware, there are only 11 premier etages in the state of comparable size and only two that are larger. Thus the house is important for its sheer magnitude as an example of the Creole tradition.

Reserve is especially important because of its early decorative detailing. Although the Creole tradition dates to the earliest days of the Louisiana colony, most of the extant examples are from the mid-nineteenth century. As far as the State Historic Preservation Office is aware, Reserve is one of only about 20 Creole houses in the state which feature significant pre-Greek Revival decorative details. These include four exceptional Federal wraparound mantels and various window and door surrounds.

Finally, three of the four mantels at Reserve make conspicuous use of the French lozenge motif. This French Renaissance detail is important, but it appears only on a very small minority of relatively early Creole houses (the NHL Madame John's Legacy, for instance).

The following is extracted from a typescript history of Reserve Plantation prepared by Michael J. Maurin, presently with St. John the Baptist Parish Library and formerly superintendent of the Godchaux-Henderson Sugar Refinery:

"Part of the property that would become the extensive Reserve Plantation was settled in the 1760s by Jean Baptiste Laubel (Lobel) and his wife Marie Therese Fontenot. Jean Baptiste died in 1774, but his widow continued on the land. After the Louisiana Purchase, the U.S. government confirmed the land claim of Jean Baptiste, Jr. and Louis Laubel. The land was six arpents fronting the Mississippi by forty arpents deep. Louis and Jean Baptiste, Jr., split the land into two equal size tracts which they sold individually in 1809.

"The next known owners are Francois and Elisee Rillieux, brothers who were part of Louisiana's large free people of color population. It seems likely that the Rillieux brothers were responsible for the Federal period remodeling and enlarging of the house. In 1822 they began purchasing small adjacent tracts of land and consolidating them into a sugar plantation. They formed a "societe" (company or partnership) to operate their holdings on May 11, 1825. The Rillieux brothers amassed a plantation with a 14 and ¼ arpent front. Francois became sole owner, and on his death an auction of his plantation and mill was held.

"The new owners were Antoine Boudousquie and his brother-in-law, Michel T. Andry. They formed a "societe" on March 23, 1833. By 1849–50, as noted in Champomier's *Statement of the Sugar Crop,* Boudousquie was sole owner. In Champomier's 1850–51 compilation the plantation is listed as Reserve. Boudousquie died November 25, 1855. His widow, Sophie Andry, representing also her children, continued operation of the plantation. Bankruptcy forced Mrs. Boudousquie to sell the plantation on June 1, 1869, to Leon Godchaux. At this time the property had a 19¼ arpent depth. Of course, it took some time for the plantation to get back on a sound economic footing after the disruptive Civil War and Reconstruction years. However, by 1893, Godchaux had doubled the size of the plantation. *The Daily States* of New Orleans, in its November 28, 1894, issue describing a visit to Godchaux's "famous Reserve Plantation," referred to him as "one of the largest sugar planters in the South." The huge sugar mill's capacity was emphasized in the article, with no reference made to the main house. The Godchaux family continued to own the plantation until the 1950s."

SCOTLANDVILLE (East Baton Rouge Parish) *District 6, Southern University campus*

Southern University Archives Building

The Southern University Archives Building is significant in the areas of education and black history because it was the first building on the Southern University, Baton Rouge campus and as such is a visual reminder of the institution's establishment in Scotlandville in 1914.

In 1879, Pinckney B. S. Pinchback, T. T. Allain, and Henry Demas sponsored the movement in the Louisiana State Constitutional Convention that resulted in the establishment, in the city of New Orleans, of an institution "for the education of persons of color." This institution was chartered as Southern University in January 1880 by the General Assembly of the State of Louisiana. A 1912 legislative act authorized the closing and sale of the university and its reestablishment on a new site.

On March 9, 1914, Southern University was opened in Scotlandville, Louisiana, under the presidency of Dr. Joseph Samuel Clark. What is now called the Southern University Archives Building was the only habitable building on the site. This structure served many functions, including a home for the president and his family, conference center, office of the president and his assistants, girls' dormitory, dining hall, hospital, social center, and meeting place for the University Council. As such it was the focus of campus activity for several years. When Dr. G. Leon Netterville, President Emeritus of Southern University, came to the school in 1921, he remembers the house as being the "busiest place" on campus.

SHREVEPORT (Caddo Parish)   *1057 Texas Ave., District 4*
Antioch Baptist Church

The Antioch Baptist Church is significant in the area of architecture for two reasons: (1) It represents the work of a prolific master. The architect was N. S. Allen, F.A.I.A., Shreveport's first true architect and Louisiana's first Fellow of the American Institute of Architects. In 1870 Allen came to Shreveport to practice architecture. During the final third of the nineteenth century he designed over 300 buildings and literally changed the skyline of Shreveport. It is known that there are only two other examples of Allen's work remaining in Shreveport. (2) It is an architectural landmark among black churches in Louisiana because of its pronounced Romanesque Revival articulation. There is probably no other period black church in Louisiana whose design followed "high style" trends as closely, as competently, or as elaborately as Antioch did. It must be noted in this regard that most old black churches across the state are humble, unpretentious structures with little or no styling. In addition, it is probably the only historic black church in the state designed by the acknowledged leading architect of a major urban area.

The Antioch Baptist Church was organized in 1866 when seventy-three newly freed blacks secured letters of honorable dismissal from the First Baptist Church (white) and formed the First Colored Baptist Church. In 1871, the congregation changed its name to Antioch Baptist Church. The present church building was completed in 1903.

SHREVEPORT (Caddo Parish)   *1627 Weinstock St.*

Central High School

Central High School is of local educational significance because it was the first high school for blacks in Shreveport and their only high school until 1949.

Until Central began operating in September of 1917, there was no opportunity for Shreveport's black population to receive a high school education. The school filled an even greater need because it drew students from surrounding parishes and East Texas. The students boarded in Shreveport during the week in various rooming houses in the neighborhood. Apparently, it was also a common practice for local families to let out a room to a student. The school grew from a student body of 144 in 1919 to over 1,600 in 1940. There were fourteen students in the first graduating class (1919) and 215 in 1940. Central graduated its last class in 1949, and the newly built Booker T. Washington High School assumed its role. Central became a junior high at that time and is now an elementary school.

SHREVEPORT (Caddo Parish)   *Southwest of Central Business District*

St. Paul's Bottoms Historic District
"Ledbetter Heights"

The St. Paul's Bottoms Historic District is significant in the area of architecture as a superior example of a late nineteenth to early twentieth century working-class neighborhood within the context of Louisiana.

The Bottoms contains architectural types which, taken together, form a good example of a typical late nineteenth to early twentieth century working-class neighborhood of the Deep South. This is important because historic working-class areas have often been the targets of highway projects or urban renewal efforts. Hence, few such areas survive in Louisiana with any degree of cohesive character. The Bottoms is thought to be the largest period working-class area in the state outside New Orleans. At one time, areas like the Bottoms existed in other Louisiana cities such as Baton Rouge and Alexandria. But these areas are now fragmented and take the form of isolated pockets rather than continuous neighborhoods.

The importance of the Bottoms can be seen in its collection of shotgun houses. The shotgun house in its various forms is considered the hallmark of working-class housing in the Deep South. With over 560 shotgun houses, the Bottoms has what is thought to be the largest collection of any neighborhood in Louisiana except for New Orleans. Unlike in New Orleans, however, the shotgun houses in the Bottoms are mainly single, and there are no camelbacks and very few side halls. Hence, the shotgun houses in the Bottoms are much closer to the rural antecedents of the type than the more urbane and developed shotgun houses of New Orleans. Consequently, they can be said to better represent the traditional shotgun working-class house type. Given this, and given the large number of shotgun houses in the Bottoms, it is fair to say that the Bottoms represents, at least in one sense, Louisiana's most important collection.

But the significance of the Bottoms is not solely dependent upon its shotgun houses. There are also bungalows, cottages, shops, and churches along with a goodly number of frame residences of no particular architectural type. These also help form the district's overall humble, unpretentious, working-class character. This character is impressive because of its cohesive quality and integrity. With only nine percent intrusions and almost no alteration of historic buildings, the Bottoms remains one of the state's best preserved historic working-class areas.

St. Paul's Bottoms originally referred to a low-lying area in the vicinity of St. Paul's African Methodist Episcopal Church. Over the years, the definition of the Bottoms has expanded to encompass a much larger area. Some of the district is part of the original town of Shreveport as laid out in 1834. The remainder is part of the city's first annexation of 1871. The portion of the district north and west of the Texas and Pacific rail line . . . was once the home of Confederate Governor Henry Watkins Allen. This area became known as Allendale and developed as an appendage to the original Bottoms neighborhood. Allendale is included within the district because its character is identical to that of the Bottoms and because it is part of the same general working-class area.

Most of the district's growth occurred after 1900. This growth was spurred by the cotton depression of the early twentieth century which caused additional black immigration into the area. The old city building permit logs show the type of construction which was taking place in the Bottoms. For example, the log for June 1922 shows that the average house for whites cost seven times the average house for blacks. In that month the average cost for a black housing unit was $558. These rented for as little as five dollars per month. Even so, the rent would pay back the cost of construction in less than ten years.

For a time the Bottoms was officially designated Shreveport's Red Light District, similar to Storyville in New Orleans. This has been seen as a result of Shreveport's heritage as a frontier town, coupled with the influence of the rivermen and saloons. In the nineteenth century, prostitution and other vice activities were located throughout the downtown area. In 1903, the city fathers undertook an effort to restrict these activities. By city ordinance they designated the Bottoms a "habitation for women of immoral character"—or the official Red Light District. Apparently, many of the houses in the Bottoms were used for prostitution at one time or another. For example, the 1904 Sanborn map shows a number of small houses marked "F.B."—an abbreviation for "female boarders." A few large and pretentious "bawdy houses" were built in the district, but the last of them burned in 1975. In 1917, the Red Light District status of the Bottoms was revoked by referendum. This certainly represented a moralist effort, but there was another consideration. With the nation preparing for World War I, there was no chance the Army would locate a base near Shreveport if the city had a Red Light District.

In the 1920s the district became an entirely black area, as it is to this day. As the original owners of much of the district's rental property passed on, there was a proliferation of heirs, each of whom owned a fraction of what were once much larger holdings. This phenomenon worked against improving or even maintaining the district's housing stock. But it also helped to preserve the district in a good state of integrity.

SPRINGFIELD (Livingston Parish)   *At dead end of SH 1038*
The Carter Plantation

As an early nineteenth-century house which was built by a free black man and lived in by an important local political figure, the Carter House is significant in the areas of black history and politics/government. It also has a degree of architectural significance.

The Carter House is situated on property acquired by James Rheem under a Spanish land grant in 1804. In about 1817, a free black man named Thomas Freeman acquired the land. Freeman's ownership and residence in the house are documented in a commissioner's report issued in 1820, which states, "Thomas Freeman is entitled to a section of land, situated in the Parish of Saint Helena on which he now resides as an actual settler by purchase from James Rheem." The existence of such a report strongly suggests that Freeman built the extant house, since "commissioner's reports" were issued only in cases in which a person had resided on and improved the land in question.

According to an article in the *Hammond Vindicator* published as part of their Bicentennial series on "Bloody Tangipahoa," Freeman was the first black man to record a legal transaction in the Greensburg District of east Louisiana. A logical extension of this statement is that Freeman was the first black man to own property in what is now Livingston Parish. The article states also that Freeman was a man of considerable substance and owned a large amount of property. The 1830 Census lists Freeman as the head of a household of free blacks consisting of two adults and five children.

In 1838 Freeman sold the land (including the house) to W. L. Breed, an important local political figure. Breed had been sheriff of St. Helena Parish when Livingston Parish was created in 1832. By 1835 he was state representative from Livingston, the first to represent the parish. He was elected state representative again in 1841 and regained the office of sheriff of Livingston Parish in 1843. The 1840 Census lists Breed as head of a household consisting of eleven white persons and 54 black slaves.

Breed died of pleurisy at Carter House on November 7, 1843. His obituary states that he was still sheriff and concludes, "The deceased was a true Republican and an honest man and at the time of his death, not only his parish but the state sustained a severe loss."

Subsequent to Breed's ownership, the property was acquired by George Richardson, a prominent planter and direct ancestor to the present owners. Richardson lived at Carter House until his death in 1858. His descendants have occupied the house and owned the property continually since that time.

Among the prominent members of the family to be connected with the house were: Judge Marcus Tulius Carter, an early circuit judge for the Greensburg district; William Buckner Rownd, an early surveyor of Livingston Parish; Marcus Carter Rownd, a prominent local attorney; Simpson Harvey Sharp, Sheriff and Clerk of Court for Livingston Parish.

The house and grounds are still in the process of restoration by the present owners, Wiley H. Sharp, Jr. and Beverly Sharp Burgess, who hope to complete the task by the Parish Jubilee in 1980 [as of date of nomination submitted to National Register of historic places]. Mrs. Burgess lives in the house with her two children Margaret and John, Jr., and her husband, the Honorable John R. Burgess, Sr., a practicing attorney in Livingston and city judge for the town of Walker.

The Carter House also enjoys a degree of architectural significance as a local example of a raised plantation house. Because of the modifications, architectural noteworthiness rests primarily upon some fine details. These include the federal dormers, scored stucco, and the mantels.

WALLACE (St. John the Baptist Parish) *SH 18, near town*
Evergreen Plantation

Evergreen Plantation is significant in the history of American agriculture as one of the largest and most intact plantation complexes in the South. It enjoys particular distinction among this select group because fully four-fifths of the buildings are antebellum and because of the survival of the double row of twenty-two slave cabins. National significance has been chosen because the plantation system represents a significant chapter in the history of American agriculture. Circa 1930 was chosen as the ending date for agricultural significance because at about that time Evergreen ceased to be an agricultural enterprise. The buildings and plantation were abandoned from the beginning of the Depression until 1944, when Matilda Gray purchased the property. The main house is also being nominated on the state level in the area of architecture because it is one of Louisiana's grand Great River Road plantation mansions.

Plantation agriculture has its origins in India in the eighth century. Since that time "plantation regions" have developed in North Africa and various parts of the New World. In the continental United States, our plantation region comprises the old Confederacy plus some adjoining states. Plantations are an important aspect of American agricultural history, being distinct from Jeffersonian yeoman farms, manorial estates of the Hudson River and similar areas, and ranches and missions of the West. A plantation revolves around a cash crop grown on a large scale for profit. A successful plantation region requires: (1) fertile, easily tilled land available in large units; (2) abundant, landless, and cheap rural labor; (3) bulk reduction and preliminary processing techniques; (4) abundant, cheap transportation; and (5) a network of factors and factoring houses to market cash crops to other regions of the world. All these were present in the American South during the antebellum period. The plantation system continued to dominate Southern agriculture (in a modified form) in the postbellum period and on into the twentieth century.

Although the phrase "southern plantation" conjures up all sorts of images, the truth of the matter is that little remains to provide a true picture of what one was like. Plantations were noted for their large number of buildings—in effect, a world within a world, or a self-contained community. As one traveler noted, "The planter has a building for everything." However, in the overwhelming majority of cases, only the great house survives today. Plantation complexes with a significant complement of outbuildings are rare, especially when one considers the thousands that once existed. Phone interviews with senior State Historic Preservation Office staff members in other southern states revealed that the typical complex, where it exists, might have six to ten buildings. By contrast, Evergreen has thirty-seven historic buildings, including its "big house," what may be its overseer's house, two *pigeonniers,* two garconnieres, two substantial brick cottages of unknown use, a privy, and a double row of twenty-two slave cabins. It and a handful of other good-size complexes are all that is left to show someone what a plantation looked like. Evergreen enjoys particular distinction among the few surviving large plantation complexes in the South because of its large number of antebellum buildings. Almost all of the few large complexes that do survive are late nineteenth century. Finally, Evergreen is particularly distinguished by its double row of twenty-two slave cabins. While thousands upon thousands of these buildings once existed across the South, they are today exceedingly rare. Typically, a state might have maybe six or so surviving examples, with one on one plantation, two on another, etc. The standard row arrangement seen at Evergeen, while once the norm across the South, is virtually unheard of today. Only about nine plantations retain what could be considered slave row. Of these, all are in the five- to ten-house range except for Evergreen.

Evergreen is significant in the area of architecture at the state level because it is one of Louisiana's grand Great River Road plantation mansions. These "Gone With the Wind" houses lined the River Road on the eve of the Civil War, but many more have been lost over the years than have survived.

Architecturally, Louisiana is best known for its fine collection of French Creole houses and grand Greek Revival plantation houses. The state's most famous and recognizable group of monumental Greek Revival plantation "big houses" is found on the historic River Road. These homes, built by immensely wealthy sugar planters, were the absolute apex of the Greek Revival style in Louisiana. They may be briefly characterized as two-story mansions with broad double galleries (sometimes encircling the house) and monumental columns or pillars which rise to the roofline in one continuous shaft. No one will ever know the exact number of these houses that were built, but available evidence demonstates that they were once quite numerous. Many of the grandest examples were destroyed in the twentieth century and are well documented in photographs. Today, only eight major Greek Revival plantation houses remain on the River Road.

Index

Abbeville, 2
Abita Springs, 2
Acadia Parish, 29, 78
Acadian settlers, 14, 21, 61, 87, 88, 91, 93
Afton Villa, 11
Albany, 2
Alexandria, 2–10, 97–100
　first church at, 9
　first steamboat at, 5
　national cemetery at, 4
　peacetime training maneuvers at, 6
　railroad at, 5
Alexandria Daily Town Talk, 2–3, 7
Alexandria Library, 3
Alexandria National Cemetery, 4
Algiers, 10
All Saints Episcopal Church, 30
Allard Plantation, 65
Allen, Sgt. Abe, 53
Allen Parish, 48
Allendale Plantation, 76
Amite, 10
Ancient Anilco, 47
Antioch Baptist Church, 143
Arabi, 10
Architecture, Creole, 38, 39, 47, 49, 57, 105–107, 125–127, 141, 149

Arizona Academy Site, 42–43
Armant, Col. Leopold L., 91
Ascension Catholic Church, 31
Ascension Parish, 18–19, 30, 31–32, 38–39, 77, 109–111, 112–113
Ashland, 30
Assumption Parish, 14, 48, 61, 89
Athens, 10
Attakapa Militia, 60
Audubon, John James, 85
Audubon Memorial, 85
Audubon Park, 11
Avery Island, 11
Avoyelles Parish, 15, 18, 26, 28, 34, 56, 57–58, 82, 107–109, 120–122

Back Brusly Oak, 18
Badin-Roque House, 61
Bailey's Dam, 72
Bains, 11
Baker, 100–101
Baldwin, 11
Banks, Gen. Nathaniel, 3, 5, 10, 15, 35, 40, 56, 76, 82, 112, 136–138
Barataria, 11–12
Barataria Settlement, 11
Bastrop, 12

Baton Rouge, 12–13, 101–105
　site of sugar and cotton plantations, 13
　state capital at, 12
　sugar granulating at, 13
Battle of Bisland, 15
Battle of Des Allemands, 31
Battle of Franklin, 36
Battle of Mansfield, 40, 47, 50, 56, 88, 91, 112
Battle of Mansura, 56
Battle of New Orleans, 10, 23
Battle of Port Hudson, 136–140
Battle of Yellow Bayou, 82
Bayou Folk Museum, 25
Bayou Goula, 14
Bayou Lafourche, 14, 89
Bayou Manchac, 13, 77
Bayou Sara, 85
Bayou Tech, 63
Bayougoula Village, 91
Bayside Plantation, 45
Beau Pre, 45
Beaubassin, 21
Belle Chasse, 14
Bellevue, 14
Belmont Plantation, 63–64
Bennett and Cane Trading Post, 78
Bermuda, 105–107

Bernice, 14
Berwick, 15
Bienville, Gov. Jean
    Baptiste, 14, 17, 39,
    41, 51, 55, 62, 65, 68,
    70, 71, 72, 83, 89
Bienville Parish, 22
Bienville's Plantation, 65
Big Bend, 15
Bisland, 15
Black Academy at Mt.
    Olive Baptist
    Church, 71
Bocage Plantation, 18
Bogalusa, 16
    largest man-made forest
    at, 16
    largest sawmill site, 16
Bolton, James Wade, home
    of, 4–5
Bonnet Carre Crevasse, 52
Bontemps, Arna Wendell,
    home of, 97–99
Bore Plantation, 11. 66
Bossier City, 16
Bossier Parish, 14, 16
Bossier Parish Court, 14
Bossier Shed Road, 16
Boutte, 17
Bowie, James, 50, 57,
    71, 92
Bowie Residence, site of, 71
Braithwaite, 17
Braithwaite, English
    Turn, 17
Brashear, Dr. Walter, 60
Breaux Bridge, "crawfish
    capital of the
    world," 17
Bridge City, 17
Broussard, 17–18
Brusly, 18
Bunkie, 18, 107–109
Burnside, 18–19, 109–111
Burtville, 19

Cabahanoce Plantation, 43
Caddo Agency House, 79

Caddo Lake, 19
Caddo Lake, first over-
    water oil well, 19
Caddo Parish, 19, 26, 33,
    71, 78–82, 143–146
Caddo-Pine Island Field,
    first oil well in, 19
Caffery, Donelson, 36
Calcasieu Parish, 30, 50, 89
Caldwell Parish, 26–27
Calumet Plantation, 78
Camp Beauregard, 20
Camp Claiborne, 20, 21
    home of U.S. Army's
    34th Infantry
    Division, 21
Camp Livingston, 20, 21
    home of U.S. Army's
    32nd Infantry
    Division, 21
Camp Moore, 89
Camp Polk, 20
Camp Pratt, site of, 84
Canary Islanders, 11, 14,
    38–39, 64, 85
Cane-Bennett Bluff, 79
Canebrake, 114–116
Cannes Brulees, 47
Carencro, 21
Carmel, 22
Carollton, 70
Carter Plantation, 146–147
Carville, 22
Castor, 22
Catahoula Parish, 42, 47
Cathedral of St. John the
    Evangelist, 49
Cemeteries, 4, 33, 47, 58,
    74, 86, 89
Centenary College of
    Louisiana, 79
Centerville, 22
Central High School, 144
Chachahoula, 22
Chalmette, 23
Chalmette Plantations, 23
Chartier Concession, 58
Cheneyville, 23–24

Cherie Quarters Cabins,
    135–136
Chopin, Kate, home of, 25
Christ Episcopal Church,
    Covington, 29
Christ Episcopal Church,
    Napoleonville, 61
Church of the Holy Cross
    Episcopal, 79
Church of the Incarnation, 10
Churches (see individual
    listings)
City of Slidell
    Centennial, 83
Civil War, 4, 5–6, 7, 8–9,
    10, 11, 12, 13, 14, 15,
    17, 22, 31, 32, 35, 36,
    39, 40, 42, 43, 45, 47,
    48, 50, 51, 53, 56, 57,
    58, 60, 76, 77, 79, 80,
    81, 82, 84, 86, 88, 89,
    91, 112, 136–140
Claiborne Parish, 10, 42–43
Claiborne Parish Court
    House, 43
Clarence, 24
Clayton, prehistoric city
    at, 24
Clinton, 24–25
Clinton Courthouse, 24
Cloutierville, 25–26
Coates Bluff, 26, 70
Cocoville, 26
Coincoin, Marie Therese,
    home of, 105–107
Colfax, 26
Colfax Riot, 26
Colonial Gateway
    Corral, 62
Columbia, 26–27
Concordia Parish, 24, 34,
    92, 114–116
Confederate Cemetery, 47
Confederate Girl's Diary,
    A, 53
Confederate Ironclad
    Missouri, 80
Confederate Navy Yard, 80

Congo Square, 123–124
Convent, 27–28
  town of, 27
Corps d'Afrique, 137
Cottage, home of Thomas
  Butler, 85–86
Cotton industry, 5, 13, 44,
  64, 69, 87, 93, 99–100,
  111–112, 115
Cottonport, 28
Covington, 29
Cradle of the Mexican
  War, 56
Crowley, 29

Darrow, 30
de la Ronde House, 23
de Soto, Hernando,
  discoverer of
  Mississippi River,
  34, 47
de Tonti, Henri, 14, 62
Degas, Edgar, French
  impressionist
  painter, 66
Denham Springs, 30
DeQuincy, 30
Derry, 111–112
Des Allemands, 31
Desfosse House, 56
DeSoto Parish, 22, 47, 54,
  56, 88
Destrehan, 31
Destrehan Manor House, 31
Dillard, James H., home of,
  128–131
Dodd College, 80
Donaldsonville, 31–32,
  112–113
  former state capital at, 32
  second Acadian Coast, 31
Dorseyville, 113–114
Doyline, 32
Drake's Salt Works, 39
Dubach, 33
Dugat, Pierre, homesite
  of, 50
Dupree, Rev. John, 58

Earl Williamson Park, 33
Early Cattle Industry, 93
Early Spanish Missions, 95
East Baton Rouge Parish,
  12–13, 19, 77, 78,
  100–105, 136–140,
  142–143
East Carroll Parish, 51, 78
East Feliciana Parish,
  24–25, 44, 53
East Louisiana State
  Hospital, 44
Edgard, 33
Elton, 33
Embrick, Lt. Gen. Stanley
  D., 6
English Manchac, 19
English Turn, 17
Enterprise Plantation, 72
Epps, 33–34
Epps, Edwin, home of,
  107–109
Epps House, 18
Erwinville, 34
Eunice, 34
Evan Hall Slave Cabins,
  112–113
Evangeline, 21, 88
Evangeline Oak, 88
Evangeline Parish, 92
Evergreen, 34
Evergreen Plantation,
  148–149

False River, 51
Fashion Plantation, 40
Faubourg Marigny Historic
  District, 125–127
Feliciana Courthouse, 44
Ferriday, 34, 114–116
Filhiol House, site of, 94
First Acadian Settlers in
  Louisiana, site of, 87
First American force sent to
  the European theater, 21
First Bowie knife, 57
First Caddo Parish
  courthouse, 80

First chapel in
  Louisiana, 14
First [Protestant]
  church, 37
First county training school
  in South, 116–118
First electrocution, site
  of, 22
First granulated sugar, 13
First highway through New
  Orleans, 68
First mass in French
  Louisiana, 92
First mayor of New
  Orleans, 11
First missionary martyr, 32
First oil refinery, 46
First oil well, 46
First oil well in North
  Louisiana, 19
First over-water oil well, 19
First rock salt mine, 11
First school in Washington
  Parish, 37
First United Methodist
  Church, Columbia,
  26–27
First United Methodist
  Church, Pineville,
  73–74
First United Methodist
  Church, Slidell, 83
First Ward Justice
  Courthouse and
  Jail, 10
First water travel route to
  New Orleans, 51, 67
First white settlement, 72
Fisher, 35
Flagville, 40
Flint-Goodridge Hospital of
  Dillard University,
  127–128
Fontainebleau, 55
*Forgotten People: Cane
  River's Creoles of
  Color, The,* 107
Fort Beauregard, 42

Fort Brashear, 60
Fort Claiborne, site of, 63
Fort De La Boulaye, 72
Fort De Russy, 57
Fort Humbug, 81
Fort Jackson, 92
Fort Jesup, 56
Fort Miro, 59
Fort Pike, 83
Fort Polk, 35
Fort Selden, site of, 63
Fort St. Charles, 66
Fort St. Jean Baptiste, 62
Fort St. John, 66
Fort St. Leon, 14
Forts Buhlow and
    Randolph, 35
Foster, Murphy James,
    Louisiana governor, 37
Franklin, 36–37
    Civil War battle at, 36
Franklinton, 37–38
    early Protestant
    church, 37
    Old Choctaw Trail, 38
French Settlement, 38
Fullerton, 38
Fullerton Mill and
    Town, 38

Gaines, Ernest J., birthplace
    of, 135
Galvez, 38–39
Galvez, Bernardo, Spanish
    governor, 14, 19, 39,
    60, 64, 85
Galveztown, 38–39
Garden District, 66–67
Gates, Frederick Larned, 64
German settlers, 31, 40, 48,
    58, 59, 70, 87, 91, 126
Germantown Colony, 59
Gibson, 39
Gibson Methodist Episcopal
    Church, 39
Godchaux-Reserve
    Plantation House,
    141–142

Goldonna, 39
Goldsmith-Godchaux
    House, 67
Grace Episcopal
    Church, 86
Grace Memorial Episcopal
    Church, 41
Gramercy, 39
Grand Coteau, 39
Grant, Gen. Ulysses S., 51
Grant Parish, 26
Grant's Canal, 51
Grave of Unknown
    Confederate
    Soldier, 58
Great Raft, 81
Greensburg, 39–40
Gretna, city of, 40
Hadrian, Roman Emperor,
    sculpture of, 64
Hahnville, 40
Hall, Luther E., 12
Hammond, 40–41
    "Strawberry Capital of
    America," 40
    walnut tree derivative
    from George
    Washington's Mt.
    Vernon, 41
Hammond, Peter, 41
Hand-planted forest, 16
Harahan, 41
Harrisonburg, 42
Hart, Lt. Com. John E.,
    tomb of, 86
Harvey, 42
Harvey Canal, 42
Harvey Castle Site, 42
Haynes Settlement, 84–85
Hebron Baptist Church, 43
Highland Road, 13
Historic Oaks of
    Cottonport, 28
Holden, 42
Holly Grove Methodist
    Church, 53
Holy Rosary Institute,
    118–119

Holy Trinity Catholic
    Church, 81
Home Place, 54
Homer, 42–43
Hopedate Sugar Mill, 23
Hotel Bentley, 6
Houma, 43
Houmas House, 18
Houmas Landing, 90
Hungarian settlement, 53
Hymel, 43–44
Hypolite Bordelon
    House, 57

Iberia Parish, 11, 45, 63–65,
    84
Iberville, Pierre, 13, 51, 58,
    67, 68, 70, 77, 78, 90,
    92
Iberville Parish, 14, 22, 76,
    78, 87, 113–114
Independence, town of, 44
Indian Camp Plantation, 22
Indian Museum, 57
Indian Village, 59, 83
Inglewood Plantation
    Historic District,
    99–100
Innis, 44
International Boundary
    Marker, 54
Isles Dernieres, 43
Italian settlement, 44

Jackson, 44
    first permanent mental
    hospital at, 44
Janesville, site of, 45
Jeanerette, 45
    Bayside Plantation, 45
    Beau Pre, 45
    Nicolas Provot, town
    "father," 45
Jefferson, 45
Jefferson City, 67
Jefferson Davis Parish, 33,
    46, 93
Jefferson Island, 46

Jefferson Parish, 11, 17, 41,
43, 45–46, 47–48,
58–59, 70
Jennings, 46
first oil well, 46
first refinery, 46
Jewish Cemetery, 74
Jonesville, 47

Kansas City Southern
Depot, 30
Keachi College, 56
Keachie, 47
Kees Park, 74
Kenner, 47–48
birthplace of first native-
born governor, 48
plantation dependency
at, 47
Kenner Town Hall, 47
Kent Plantation House, 6
Kentwood, 48, 116–118
Killona, 48
Kinder, 48

L'ansse Aux Outardes, 70
L'Hermitage, 19
La Providence, 48
La Salle, claim to
Louisiana, 68
Labadieville, 48
Labarre Road, 59
Labranche Plantation
Dependency, 47
Lacombe, 49
Lacoste Plantation, 23
LaCour, 49
LaCour Store, 49
Lafayette, 49–50, 118–119
first Parish church, 49
site of Indian artifacts, 50
Lafayette Museum, 49
Lafayette Parish, 17–18, 21,
49–50, 118–119
Lafayette Square, 67
Lafitte, Pierre Boitte, grave
of, 22

Lafitte, Jean, 41, 50
Lafourche Parish, 90
Lafreniere Plantation, 41
Lake Bistineau, 32
Lake Charles, 50
Lake Pontchartrain, 51, 67
Lake Providence, 51
Lakeland, 51
Land's End Plantation, 88
Lane's Ferry, 71
LaPlace, 52
Lawyer's Row, 25
Le Chemin Militaire, 91
"Le Petit Versailles," 91
Lecompte, 119–120
Ledbetter, Huddie
"Leadbelly," blues
singer, 71
Leesville, 53
Lejeune, John Archer, 44
Leland College, 100–101
Les Allemands, German
settlement at, 48
Lincoln Parish, 33, 92
Linwood, 53
Linwood Plantation, 63
Livingston, 53
Hungarian settlement
at, 53
Livingston Parish, 2, 22, 30,
38, 42, 53, 77, 84–85,
93, 146–147
Locust Grove, 86
Logansport, international
boundary marker at, 54
Loggy Bayou, 81
Long, Huey Pierce Sr. and
Caledonia Tison, 94
Longfellow, Henry
Wadsworth, 21, 88
Loranger, 54
Loranger High School, 54
Los Adais, 62
Louisiana African-American
Heritage Sites, 96–149
Louisiana College, 75
Louisiana Historical
Markers, 1–95

Louisiana Maneuvers,
peacetime training
exercise, 6, 21
Louisiana Native Guards,
136, 138
Louisiana Purchase, oldest
settlement in, 24
Louisiana State University,
9, 12, 13
Luling, 54
Lutcher, 54–55
Perique tobacco at, 53–54

Macedonia Baptist
Church, 42
Madewood Plantation
House, 61
Madisonville, town of, 55
Magnolia Lane, 17
Magnolia Plantation,
111–112
Maison de Marie Therese,
105–107
Malarcher House
Marker, 27
Mandeville, 55
state park at, 55
Manning, Thomas
Courtland, 7
Mansfield, 56
Mansura, 56, 120–122
battle at, 56
Many, 56–57
Cradle of the Mexican
War, 56
Marksville, 57–58
Confederate stronghold
at, 57
first Bowie knife, 57
prehistoric native tribes
site, 57–58
Marksville Site, 58
Marthaville, 58
Martin, 58
Mater, James, 54
Maurepas Island, 58
McCallum House, 136–140

McKinley High School, 101–102
Melrose Plantation, 107, 122
Metairie, 58–59
Metairie and Gentilly Ridges, 68
Minden, 59
    German settlement site, 59
Monroe, 59, 123
    native tribe site at, 59
    stockade site at, 59
Montepelier, 60
Montz, Armand Sr., 52
Moore, Thomas Overton, 10
Morehouse Parish, 12
Morehouse Parish Training School, 12
Morgan City, 60
    early militia at, 60
    Union fort at, 60
Mouton, Gen. Alfred, 50
Mt. Carmel Academy, 64
Mt. Olivet Episcopal Church, 76
Mt. Vernon Walnut, 41

Napoleonville, 61
Natchez Trace, The, 24
Natchitoches, 24, 61–63
    former capital of the Province of Texas, 62
    fort sites at, 63
    oldest permanent settlement in Louisiana Purchase, 61
Natchitoches Parish, 24, 25–26, 39, 58, 61–63, 105–107, 111–112, 122
National Hansen's Disease Center, 22
Native tribes, 2, 11, 14, 18, 26, 33–34, 38, 39, 40, 41, 47, 49, 50, 55, 57–58, 59, 62, 63, 68, 79, 83, 87, 89, 90, 91, 93
New Iberia, 63–65
    important waterway at, 63
    pioneer trail at, 65
    sculpture at, 64
    settlement of, 64
    sugar production at, 63–64
New Orleans, 65–70, 123–134
    African-American health care in, 127–128
    christening of territory, 68
    distinctive architectural area of, 125–127
    early homes and gardens, 66–67
    first highway through city, 68
    first sighting of, 68
    first steamboat to successfully navigate rivers, 69
    first water travel route to city, 67
    focal point for African-Americans, 123–124
    oldest street railway line, 69
    oldest surviving church, 68
    painting site of French impressionist Edgar Degas, 66
    public square for city's first suburb, 67
    red-light district, 69
    residence of first mayor, 66
    residence of city founder, 65
New Sarpy, 70
Newellton, 63
Nicholls, Francis Tillou, 32
    homesite of, 90

Northup, Solomon, 18, 107–109
O'Neill, Charles Austin, 36
Oak Alley Plantation, 91
Oak and Pine Alley, 88
Oak Grove, 71
Oil City, 71
Oil industry, 19, 46, 60
Old Cattle Trail, 22
Old Choctaw Trail, 38
Old City Hall, 76
Old Fenner Road, 93–94
Old Hickory, 49
Old Mortuary Chapel, 68
Old Portage, 68
Old Rapides Bank Building, 8
Old Shiloh Community, 14
Old Spanish Trail, 65
Oldest permanent settlement in Louisiana, 61
Oldest sugar cane plantation in U.S., 72
Olinkraft, 94
Opelousas, 71
    former state capital, 71
    site of Bowie residence, 71
Orange Grove, 43
Orleans Parish, 10, 11, 65–70, 123–134
Oscar, 135–136
Ouachita Parish, 59, 93–94, 123
Ouachita River Steamboat Era, 27

Parish Courthouse, 38
Pass Manchac, 55
Patoutville, 72
Patterson, 72
Patton, Maj. Gen. George, 6
Pendleton Crossing, 57
Pentagon Buildings, 13
Perique tobacco, 53–54
Perkins Ferry, 50
Phoenix, 72
Pilot House, 69

Pineville, 72–76
  city park, 74–75
  early Jewish graves at, 74
Plantations, 6, 11, 18, 23,
  27, 28, 30, 32, 40, 41,
  43, 45, 47, 49, 50, 52,
  54, 55, 60, 61, 63–64,
  65, 66, 72, 76, 78, 84,
  86, 88, 91, 99,
  105–107, 111–112,
  114–116, 122,
  125–127, 141–142,
  146–147, 148–149
Plaquemine, old city hall
  at, 76
Plaquemines Parish, 14, 17,
  72, 77, 92
Poche, Judge Felix Pierre,
  home of, 27
Point Pleasant, 12
Pointe Coupee, 51
Pointe Coupee Parish, 34,
  44, 49, 51, 135–136
Ponchatoula, 76
Ponchatoula Depot, 76
Poplar Chapel A.M.E.
  Church, 140–141
Port Allen, 76
Port Barre, 77
Port Hudson, 77, 136–140
Port Hudson Battlefield,
  136–140
Port Sulphur, hub of state's
  sulphur industry, 77
Port Vincent, 77
Porter, Alexander, 36
Pouppeville, 78
Poverty Point, site of
  prehistoric culture,
  33–34
Prairieville, 77
Presentation Academy, 26
Prince Hall Masonic
  Temple, 102–103
Provot, Nicolas, 45

Randall Oak, 34

Rapides Parish, 2–10,
  20–21, 23–24, 35,
  72–76, 97–100,
  119–120
  governors of, 8–9
Rayne, 78
Rayville, 140–141
Red River Parish, 58
Redstick, 78
Reserve, 141–142
Rice industry, center of, 29
Richland Parish, 140–141
Roncal, 48
Roosevelt, President
  Theodore Roosevelt
  at, 78
Rosedale, 78
Rosedale Road, 76
Rosedown Plantation, 86
Rouqier, Francois, homesite
  of, 62
Rouquette, Abbe Adrien
  E., 49
Russelville, 10

Sabine Parish, 35, 56–57, 95
Saint Jacques de
  Cabahanoce, 43–44
Saint Mary Magdalen
  Church, 2
Salt industry, 11, 22, 32,
  39, 89
Sand Bar Fight, 92
Sanders, Jared Young,
  Louisiana governor, 37
Sang Pour Sang Hill, battle
  site, 26
Sarto Old Iron Bridge, 15
Scotlandville, 78, 142–143
Scott Street School,
  103–105
Second Caddo Parish
  Courthouse, 82
Shreveport, 78–82,
  143–146
  Confederate blockade
  at, 81

Confederate navy yard
  at, 80
first African-American
  high school in, 144
first courthouse at, 80
first Episcopal service
  held at, 79
founding of, 82
historic working-class
  neighborhood in,
  144–146
opening of Red River to
  navigation, 81
Simmesport, 82
Skirmish of Boutte
  Station, 17
Slave cabins, 112–113,
  135–136, 148–149
Slidell, 83–84
  centennial of, 83
  native tribes at, 83
  oldest Methodist
  assembly in city, 83
Slidell Town Hall and
  Jail, 84
Smith, Gen. E. Kirby,
  residence of, 81
Soldiers' Rest, 51
Sorrel, 84
Southdown, 84
Southdown Plantation
  House, 84
Southern University, 78
Southern University
  Archives Building,
  142–143
Spanish Lake, 65, 84
Spanish Manchac, 19
Springfield, 84–85,
  146–147
St. Andrew's Episcopal
  Church, 25
St. Bernard, 85
St. Bernard Parish, 10,
  23, 85
St. Cecilia School, 17
St. Charles Borromeo "Little
  Red Church," 31

St. Charles Line, 69
St. Charles Parish, 17, 31,
  40, 48
St. Emma Plantation, 32
St. Francis Xavier Cathedral
  Complex, 9
St. Francisville, 85–87
  John James Audubon
    at, 85
  native tribes at, 87
  one of south's earliest
    railroads at, 87
  one of state's oldest
    Protestant churches
    at, 86
  river port at, 85
St. Gabriel, 87
St. Helena Parish,
  39–40, 60
St. James, 87
St. James A.M.E. Church,
  131–132
St. James Parish, 27–28,
  43–44, 54–55, 87, 91
St. James United Methodist
  Church, 123
St. John Baptist Church,
  Dorseyville, 113–114
St. John Baptist Church,
  Lecompte, 119–120
St. John the Baptist Catholic
  Church, 33
St. John the Baptist Parish,
  33, 52, 58, 141–142,
  148–149
St. John the Evangelist
  Church Parish, 65
St. John's Episcopal
  Church, 90
St. Joseph, 87
St. Joseph Catholic
  Church, 95
St. Joseph's School,
  109–111
St. Landry Parish, 34, 39,
  71, 77, 93
St. Martin Parish, 17, 88
St. Martinville, 88

St. Mary Parish, 11, 15,
  36–37, 60, 72, 84
St. Maurice, 88
St. Maurice Plantation, 88
St. Paul Lutheran Church,
  120–122
St. Paul's Bottoms Historic
  District, 144–146
St. Peter African Methodist
  Episcopal Church,
  132–134
St. Tammany Parish, 2, 29,
  49, 55, 83–84
State Seminary of Learning
  and Military
  Academy, 9
Steamer New Orleans, 69
Stonewall, 88
Storyville, 69
Strand Theatre, 82
Sugar industry, 11, 13, 23,
  28, 32, 36, 45, 54, 55,
  60, 64, 66, 72, 84, 88,
  113, 142
Sugar Kettle, 13
Sugartown, 25
Sulphur, 89
Sulphur Mines, 89
Supreme, 89

Tangipahoa, 89
  Confederate training
    camp at, 89
Tangipahoa Parish, 10,
  40–41, 44, 48, 54, 55,
  76, 89, 95, 116–118
Tangipahoa Parish Training
  School, old dormitory
  at, 116–118
Taylor, Gen. Zachary, 56
Tchoupitoulas Plantation, 41
Temple Roof Garden,
  102–103
Temple Theatre, 102
Tensas Parish, 63, 87
Terre-Aux-Bouef, 85
Terrebonne Parish, 22, 39,
  43, 84

Tezcuco Plantation, 28
Thibodaux, 90
  one of oldest Episcopal
    churches in
    Mississippi
    Valley, 90
Thibodaux, Henry Schuyler,
  tomb of, 90
Third Caddo Parish
  Courthouse, 82
Thirty-first Parallel, 89
"To A Point Called Chef
  Menteur," 69
Tonti (see de Tonti, Henri)
Trenton, 94
Trinity Episcopal
  Church, 23
Tunica, 90
Twelve Years A Slave, 18,
  107–108
Twin City Gospel
  Temple, 15

Uncle Sam Plantation, 28
Union Avenue Baptist
  Church, 16
Union Parish, 14
Unionville General
  Store, 33

Vacherie, 91
  early settlement at, 91
  national historic landmark
    at, 91
  route of Civil War
    troops, 91
Vacherie de Grande
  Pointe, 54
Van Benthuysen-Elms
  Mansion, 70
Venice, 92
  first mass performed at, 92
Vermilion Parish, 2, 46
Vernon Parish, 35, 38, 53
Vidalia, 92
Vienna, 92

Vieux Carre Forts, 70
Ville Platte, 92

Walker, 93
Wallace, 148–149
Washington, 93
Washington Parish, 16,
  37–38
Webster Parish, 32, 59
Wedell-Williams Airport,
  site of, 45–46
Welch, 93
West Baton Rouge Parish,
  18, 76

West Carroll Parish, 33–34,
  45, 71
West Feliciana, 93
West Feliciana Parish, 11,
  85–87, 90, 93
West Feliciana Railroad,
  87, 93
West Monroe, 93–94
  first pulp paper mill at, 94
White Hall Plantation, 28
William Kendrick Square,
  39–40
Williams Memorial
  Airport, 72
Winn Parish, 88, 94

Winnfield, 94
Woodland Plantation, 52
World's largest sawmill, 16
World's oldest continuously
  operated street railway
  line, 69
Wright, Salmon Lusk, 29

Zemurray Gardens, 95
Zemurray Gardens
  Lodge, 95
Zwolle, 95
  early Spanish missions
  at, 95